Surprising Stories
to
Stimulate Creativity

Mike Fleetham and Lucy Fleetham

Dedication

To our grandchildren and our grandparents

Thank you

Lots of folk have read the stories and tried out the activities.
They provided wonderful suggestions. Special thanks to:

- Pete, Alison, Abby, Ellie and Bella Davison
- Tim, Andrea, Tom and Evie Sully
- Alison Drever
- Lynne Williams
- Jonathan Green
- Holly Graff
- Ella and Arthur Fleetham.

Deep gratitude also goes to Mike Tarbell (Wahrare) of the Iroquois Indian Museum, New York State, for sharing stories from his tribe's rich heritage

Permission to photocopy

Surprising Stories to Stimulate Creativity
106522
ISBN-13: 978 1 85503 483 9
© Mike Fleetham and Lucy Fleetham
Illustrations © Fausto Bianchi and John Dillow
Cover illustration © John Dillow
All rights reserved
First published 2010
Reprinted 2011
Printed in the UK for LDA
LDA, Findel Education, Hyde Buildings, Ashton Road, Hyde, Cheshire, SK14 4SH

Contents

Introduction

About this book

This book is for educators who want to discover, value and enrich the creativity of their learners. It's a source of inspiration and also supplies straightforward classroom activities. It will help you to liven up your teaching and enhance your pupils' learning.

The twenty-eight short stories linked to twenty-eight classroom activities will stimulate creative thinking and learning. The stories and activities may be used together or separately. Each activity (lasting between 30 minutes and 2 hours) may be applied to the ever-changing knowledge, skills, attitudes and values appearing in school curricula. Each story can stand alone, for example as a thinking starter in morning assembly or an end-of-day treat.

They are divided into four categories (see p. 8):

- Creative classroom

Develop a creative learning community.

- Creative problem-solving

Innovative responses to real challenges.

- Creativity and thinking skills

Develop higher-order thinking skills.

- Creative arts

Develop creative expression through a range of media.

This book is written with teachers and primary-age children in mind, but it is not restricted to that audience. The stories are not too scary for 5-year-olds and not too boring for 11-year-olds. However, Mike has used them in training with secondary students and adults, and the activities have been applied at all school phases. There's also no reason why parents shouldn't use the stories at home to back up the creative messages being given at school.

It's a book to make sure that your children are well prepared not only to survive but to thrive in the twenty-first century. It gives you these things:

❶ practical resources for creative teaching and creative learning

❷ a no-nonsense understanding of creativity

❸ enrichment of your own personal and professional creativity

❹ ways to meet local and national requirements for a creative curriculum

❺ methods to value and enhance the creativity of all your learners

❻ knowledge to engage in a debate about twenty-first-century teaching and learning

❼ a chance to rediscover the real, unfettered joy that's possible when you're teaching and learning creatively.

Why stimulate creativity?

By the time you get to read this book, the world will be a different place from the one in which it was written. In our rapidly changing environment, personal and professional success depends more than ever on creative thinking and problem-solving. We never know what's round the corner. When interesting and unexpected things come our way, we need the tools, techniques and personal qualities to respond. And it's our duty to prepare our children in the same way. Who can say what challenges and opportunities they will face as they grow up?

This is not a revolution; it's an evolution of learning to meet the needs of a changing world. Creativity is not the next big thing to squeeze into a packed school day. Rather, it's a natural way of enriching the worthy things that schools already do. It's also a means of re-energising the people who teach and learn within their walls.

Describing creativity – 'I'm not a creative person'

A long time ago in ancient China, two generals were preparing to defend their people from a great army that had camped a little way downriver. General Po was very worried about the threat but too proud to admit it. General Zang, however, seemed calm and relaxed. You would never have guessed that ten thousand enemy soldiers were getting ready to attack him. Po was annoyed because Zang wasn't taking the situation seriously, so he challenged Zang to make 100,000 arrows and gave him four days to do it.

After the first day Zang had done nothing but stroll around the camp whistling. After the second day Zang had done nothing but soak in a hot bath singing. After the third day Zang had done nothing but lay in his tent sleeping. At the beginning of the fourth day Zang disappeared, so Po set off to find him and confront him about his laziness.

Eventually Po discovered him down by the river. He was just about to challenge him when a curious sight caught his eyes. Thirty boats were moored by the river bank and in each one sat a crew of straw dummies dressed to look like soldiers. A dense fog lay over the water as Zang gently pushed the boats off towards the enemy camp.

Po hid behind a bush to watch. A few hours later the boats returned, pulled by ropes that Zang had attached to their hulls. Embedded in each straw soldier were hundreds of enemy arrows. Zang started to pull them out and pile them up on the river bank. Before long he had collected 100,000.

Fast forward a few thousand years to April 2008 and the Guggenheim Museum, New York. Installation artist Cai Guo-Qiang and his team have variously suspended, propped, balanced, hung and laid out an assortment of installation artwork into the museum's gently upward-spiralling walkway. The exhibition is called 'I Want to Believe'. Tucked away in a blank white room off the main hallway is a boat made of wood and woven grasses. Suspended from the ceiling, it appears to hover in the air. It sprouts hundreds of white-tipped arrows and resembles a stretched-out porcupine. The piece is called *Borrowing your Enemy's Arrows*.

Creativity is at work in three different ways here:

❶ Creative thinking and problem-solving by General Zang

❷ Creative artistic interpretation of an ancient story by Cai Guo-Qiang

❸ Creative application of an experience in an art gallery by Mike Fleetham to make a point about creativity.

Have you ever heard anyone say, 'Oh, I'm not very creative'? If you have, then they're probably talking about no. 2 in the list of categories, the creative arts. More often than not, they believe themselves to be unable to draw or paint well. They may doubt their musical ability or creative imagination. Dig a little deeper and you'll find the reasons why: usually a lack of self-belief and

fear caused (sadly) by destructive and judgemental criticism from another person – 'You can't draw', 'You'll never be a singer'. It's amazing what self-limiting beliefs we adults carry from our childhood. Mike still quakes at the prospect of karaoke.

The people who believe they are not creative will most likely make their way successfully through life, unaware of the creativity they use to do so. Perhaps they combine elements of their past experience to manage a difficult personal situation. Or they may seek out new experiences or ways of doing things in response to boredom. Maybe they are creative in the kitchen, garden or workshop, or even in the bedroom. There is far more to creativity than landscape painting and musical composition. The wider our definition of creativity and our belief in ourselves as creative people, the more chance our learners have to develop their own creativity.

Creativity is not a special genetic endowment reserved for a favoured few; neither is it the objects or events it produces. Creativity is fundamentally an attitude toward life. It requires equal parts of receptivity and resourcefulness – an openness to intuitions and ideas and a readiness to put them to work. Spontaneous and disciplined, flexible and focused, the creative life is a marriage of opposites.

Laurence G. Boldt, author and career consultant

Defining creativity

I find remixing a fantastic way to kick start a creative spurt; you get all these little snippets and it's like taking something intricate to pieces and re-assembling it, but in the order and shape that you deem decent. Usually, my remixes sound absolutely nothing like the original as I tend to take one tiny fragment or theme of the original and then make up a completely new tune to fit snugly around it.

Bruce Bickerton, musician, www.alucidnation.co.uk

Pinning down an exact definition of creativity is as difficult as doing the same for quantum mechanics.

> *I think it is safe to say that no one understands Quantum Mechanics.*
>
> Richard Feynman, quantum physicist

The pinning-down metaphor is perhaps apt because if creativity were a butterfly, defining it would mean pinning it inside a display case. We'd never see its fabulous wings in action. We've chased this butterfly – into conversations, through books, across government documents and over the internet – and have found out about its wings and the way it flies.

Creativity is as much about specific thinking skills and practical skills as it is about beliefs and dispositions towards life. And the motivations to be creative may be as diverse as the products of the creative process.

Below are twelve recurring beliefs, attitudes and abilities that we discovered. In each of the story activities that follow, one or more of these themes is used as an objective. In completing all the activities each theme is encountered several times. Your children will therefore get broad and deep exposure to creativity's diverse components, and develop the essential beliefs, attitudes and abilities to be truly creative.

Creativity manifests as:

- A belief that creative potential is inside everyone and may be found everywhere
- A belief that creativity can change things and improve things
- A belief that mistakes are to be celebrated, learned from and used
- A belief that creativity can be a natural response to pain, suffering and boredom
- An attitude of positivity towards surprising and unexpected events
- An attitude of openness to new ideas and experiences when they appear
- An attitude of smart risk-taking
- An attitude of non-judgement
- An ability to seek out new ideas and experiences actively
- An ability to see familiar things in new and different ways
- An ability to use both analytic and holistic thinking
- An ability to make, think or do things that haven't been made, thought or done before.

Rather than providing you with a grid or a tick list that breaks each of these down (running the risk of providing you with a net with which to catch butterflies), may we suggest that each of these themes becomes a principle to be discovered and defined as your children carry out the tasks in this book? For example, if one activity aims to develop the skill of seeing things in a different way, as part of the debrief of the activity ask the children what they did to meet the objective. Record their thoughts as an evolving definition of this aspect of creativity. When you come back to this theme again, bring out their ideas from the previous time and take them forward.

Creativity in school

Edward de Bono distinguishes between creativity in the arts and ideas. He warns educational leaders not to think they're providing creativity in schools when they simply apply more music and dance to the curriculum. A creative curriculum is not just about painting and drawing the 8-times table, it's about inventing new and exciting ways of learning too.

If we hold a restrictive view of creativity, then children who don't excel in the arts risk developing the self-belief that they are not creative. Sir Ken Robinson describes this beautifully when he says that we must help children to discover their preferred medium (the 'substance'/'arena' with which they want to create), give them the freedom to explore it and teach them the skills to manipulate it.

Professor Howard Gardner provides us with a complete template for describing these media through his theory of Multiple Intelligences. We can argue that a child whose medium is music and who plays several instruments and composes new tunes is just as creative as one whose medium is people and who excels in building, developing and leading new teams.

When it comes to the products of creativity, we must not limit ourselves to the fruits of the creative arts such as books, paintings, plays, dances and musical performances. It is possible to have equally valuable products in other domains: creative solutions in mathematics, creative football tactics, creative experiments and questions in science and creative groupings when people work and learn together.

Children with special needs

> Creativity is now as important in education as literacy, and we should treat it with the same status.
>
> Sir Ken Robinson

When Mike teaches in special-needs schools or works with SEN groups, without fail he encounters some of the most creative minds of any classroom. It is often as if a child's special need in literacy or numeracy or behaviour has been offset by a creative gift. They may not be able to spell 'cat', but they may be able to create one adapted to the twenty-first-century. In fact many of these children are gifted when it comes to creative thinking.

More able, gifted or talented children

We need to be constantly on the look-out for creative skills, thinking and potential in all our learners. We'll no doubt discover a handful of children who excel in the various aspects of creativity. It is possible to be more able, gifted and talented in creative thinking and creative expression. See *Including Gifted, Able and Talented Children in the Primary Classroom* (LDA 2008) for ideas to identify and develop these learners.

Using this book to stimulate creativity

Each story–activity pair comes in three parts:

❶ The story

❷ Let's create – a task to enrich creativity

❸ Support, extension and application – ideas for differentiating and transferring the skills learned in the activity.

❶ The story

Get a feel for the story and plan how you will present it to your class. You could read it aloud, develop and use different voices, dress up, choose suitable background music, change the light/temperature or other environmental factors, use objects/props that appear in the story, involve the children, read outside or in a different part of school from normal, emphasise words or key moments with gestures and movements, and have colleagues jump out at appropriate moments and in surprising ways. Or log on to www.thinkingclassroom.co.uk, where you will find audio versions for some of the stories.

❷ Let's create

Each activity is presented in the following way.

Introduction

A short explanation of how the story can stimulate creativity.

Learners will create

Brief details of the product that will be created in the activity.

Learners will develop

The abilities, attitudes and beliefs of creativity (from p. 6) that learners will use and develop while making the product.

You will need

Resources and preparation needed beforehand.

Main activity

The creative task.

Plenary

Review and evaluation of the product, skills, attitudes and values.

❸ Support, extension and application

Ideas for helping younger or emerging creators, and methods for stretching older or more experienced ones, together with suggestions for using the creative activity in the broad curriculum areas.

Get in touch

If you've any comments, questions, ideas or requests, we'd love you to get in touch. Also, Mike can come to your school/business and help you stimulate your creativity – offering facilitation espresso style: new stories, strategies and extra creativity tools chosen especially for you. Details from mike@thinkingclassroom.co.uk

Lucy is the creative business manager of Thinking Classroom, and has a great deal of experience in creating systems and strategies for large organisations. Get in touch if you need a consultation about saving time and money and working in a more creative way: lucy@thinkingclassroom.co.uk

Creative classroom

The following five activities will lay the foundations for a creative learning community and a creative ethos within your class.

Story	Summary	Creative product	Creative focus
Arturo's Balloon (p. 20)	A 6-year-old boy discovers a magical balloon in his Christmas stocking	Flash box: a box with objects for generating new ideas and solving problems	Seeing in a different way Making new things Non-judgement
Foible Carrion's Curious Cabinet (p. 32)	A brilliant writer dies, leaving a locked cabinet full of unpublished work	Curious cabinet of creativity: a collection of items for kick-starting creativity and developing thinking skills	Creative potential is everywhere Seeking new ideas Smart risk-taking
Tanoma and the Snake (p. 36)	A young boy receives magical sight after being tested by a witch	Creative specs: a set of spectacles for creative looking	Seeing in a different way Creative potential is everywhere Openness to the new
The Boy who built (p. 104)	The creative imagination of a schoolboy goes unnoticed by his teacher	Class creativity charter (Triple C): a co-negotiated set of principles for developing a creative environment	Creative potential is everywhere Non-judgement
The Reluctant Wizard (p. 16)	A talented wizard is torn between helping others and following his own interests	Shower book: a creative journal for recording new ideas	Seeking new ideas Openness to the new Creative potential is everywhere Non-judgement

Creative problem-solving

The following four activities will help develop creative problem-solving

Story	Summary	Creative product	Creative focus
Alfred's Gift (p. 96)	A snow angel is banished to Earth and encounters a series of interesting problems	1. An Alfred wall 2. A creative solution	Making new things Creativity enriches life Mistakes are OK Creativity solves difficult problems
Click (p. 100)	A great magician loses 3 dangerous secrets and 3 innocent people pay a high price for his error	WHW thinking: Learning to ask, What happens when ...? to help solve problems	Creativity enriches life Smart risk-taking Creativity solves difficult problems
Rain Fairies (p. 28)	Children around the world are helped by the rain fairies	Glass Bead Game: an open-ended problem-solving technique	Seeking new ideas Using left and right brain Creativity solves difficult problems
Thinking Fairy saves the Day (p. 44)	A curious twist to a well-known story puzzle	A crazy challenge: set for others to solve	Creativity solves difficult problems Creativity enriches life Making new things

Creativity and thinking skills

The following seven activities will help develop creativity and higher order thinking skills.

Story	Summary	Creative product	Creative focus
A Tail of War (p. 12)	A frog and a snake become trapped in a never-ending struggle	Never-ending cycle: a method for using reasoning to link ideas in new ways	Seeing in a different way Making new things
Jeremy Spaniel's Golden Thoughts (p. 52)	Jeremy's tedious life is transformed when a stranger steals his thoughts	A Chevalier board: providing a simple way to create interesting questions	Creativity solves difficult problems Non-judgement Using left and right brain
The Boy who asked (p. 56)	A boy wrestles with the eternal question 'Who am I?'	101 questions: a method for generating a large number of diverse questions	Creative potential is everywhere Openness to the new Making new things
The Smallest Story on Earth (p. 118)	A young boy suffers misfortune in smaller and smaller ways	Zooms: a process for zooming in and out of any idea	Seeing in a different way Using left and right brain Creativity enriches life
The Story (p. 48)	An expert finds the ultimate story, but gets a big surprise	Story inspection: using set criteria to examine narratives	Non-judgement Using left and right brain
The Trouble with Wishes (p. 114)	Uki kills a wish devil by mistake and becomes trapped in a weird city	A wish chain: which extends thinking into a connected sequence	Positivity towards surprises Making new things Mistakes are OK
The Wizard of Burnham Market (p. 72)	A wizard loses his notebook but is remarkably unconcerned	An impossibility: to challenge thinking and clarify understanding of the possible	Creative potential is everywhere Openness to the new

Creative arts

The following twelve activities will help develop creative expression through a range of media.

Story	Summary	Creative product	Creative focus
Avani (p. 68)	The people of the planet Avani evolve with the help of alien visitors	An alien visitor: generated by a 6 x 6 grid and 2 dice	Creativity enriches life Making new things Positivity towards surprises
Four Wits of the Irish (p. 110)	A foolish young man must accept three challenges to save his lover	A 7-part retelling of the story in a choice of media	Seeing in a different way Making new things Smart risk-taking
Ghramo's Mountain (p. 108)	A stubborn man eventually reaches his goal	A new story: by the creative combination of aspects of 2 existing ones	Making new things Creative potential is everywhere
The Golden Steps (p. 24)	A greedy girl gets her come-uppance		
The Princess who could see Everything (p. 76)	A gifted princess uses incredible vision to choose her husband	A mash-up poem: about the senses, by using a grid and creative prompts	Making new things Seeing in a different way
The Hidden Gift (p. 60)	A kind woman is rewarded with an important gift	Fantasy medicines: to cure made-up childhood illnesses	Making new things Creativity enriches life Creativity solves difficult problems
The House of Loyalty (p. 88)	A city is nearly destroyed but saved in an unexpected way	PoV sketch: to bring the key element of the story to life	Creative potential is everywhere Openness to the new
The Maige Bird (p. 92)	An evil man seeks a wondrous bird and discovers its terrible secret	A maige bird and its feathers: a colourful classroom centrepiece	Making new things Creativity enriches life
The Paradigm Maverick (p. 84)	A bored girl develops special mind powers but loses her head	A PoV golem: a small clay person with a specific view of the world	Creative potential is everywhere Openness to the new Making new things
The Sparrow who swallowed a Sunset (p. 80)	A bullied sparrow dies in a desperate quest, yet is magically reborn	A clip stream: retelling the story in a series of clip-art images	Making new things Seeing in a different way
The Tale of Willy Woodknock (p. 64)	Willy gets lured into a trap by a mysterious creature	Wordplay: comparing and sorting words selected from the story	Creative potential is everywhere Using left and right brain Making new things
The Town called Est (p. 40)	A king is tricked into choosing between his town and his daughter	A 2-face: a reversible face that expresses different characteristics	Making new things

A Tail of War

A young girl from the Iroquois tribe was walking in the forest. She had nowhere to go and nothing to do, so she simply took her time enjoying the beauty of nature: the smell of pine trees, the fresh clean air, the music of birds and the soft pad-pad-pad of her moccasins on the rich earth.

All was right with the world, everything balanced, she was at peace. So, naturally, when she came to a low grassy hill in a sunlit clearing, she lay down to take a nap. She fell into a deep and dream-free sleep.

All of a sudden she woke up. A sinister grey cloud had heaved itself in front of the sun. The day turned dark and chilly and the girl began to feel uneasy. Her serenity had disappeared. She stood up and set out quickly in the direction of her village, but as she reached the top of a hill a terrible sight met her eyes: down there on the other side was the longest, shiniest, thickest, blackest snake that she had ever seen. But worse than the sight of it was what the snake was doing. It had a huge bullfrog in its mouth and was busy trying to swallow it. That was disgusting.

The snake had unhinged its jaws to create room for the frog to be pulled inside, but the frog was not making an easy meal. Its back legs had disappeared but its body was being sucked in only a little at a time. The frog was putting up a worthy fight, and as the girl watched it struggle she saw it eyeing the snake's tail, which was flicking from side to side not a bow's length away. With a desperate lunge the frog grabbed the snake's tail in its mouth and there and then began to swallow the snake.

The frog went a little farther into the snake, but at the same time the snake was being swallowed by the frog. Slowly and steadily each pulled the other into its own throat. Eventually all that was left for the girl to see was the frog's mouth full of snake and the snake's mouth full of frog. And then, with a last frantic gulp from each animal, along with a pop and a squelch, they both disappeared.

The girl stood, shocked by what she had seen. After a while the sun came out from behind that heavy grey cloud and the air turned warm again. She set off back to her village, deep in thought, and aware that she had been given a very important message about life in the world of adults.

Let's create

The story carries a powerful and relevant message about human nature. Significant themes include greed, conflict, circularity and self-destruction. Understanding the notion of 'going round in circles' is a useful preparation for adult life. Witness the number of arguments and conflicts – from personal to international – that involve two parties getting stuck in a rut, going nowhere fast. Exploit the idea of a never-ending cycle (like snake eats frog eats snake eats frog, etc.) as a creative stimulus.

Learners will create

An interesting and original never-ending cycle that meets these success criteria:

❶ It must have 2 parts (like the snake and the frog)

❷ It must have 2 creative joins that link the parts together in a never-ending loop (like the frog eating the snake eating the frog)

❸ It must have a clear connection to learning and/or an important message (in the story each animal was biting the other in order to survive, but neither did; there are no winners in war)

Learners will develop

Their ability to see things in a different way

Their ability to make things that haven't existed before

You will need

A creative environment in which diverse resources, materials and tools are easily and freely available, plus a couple of examples of never-ending cycles:

- 2 sentences, each ending with the word with which the other begins, to help practise sentence construction; e.g.:
    - Carefully she pushed open the door and peered inside.
    - Inside the old house she always walked quietly and carefully.
- 2 short musical phrases, each ending on the note with which the other begins, to create more interesting repeating phrases
- 2 numbers, each ending in the digit with which the other begins, to give a better understanding of place value and of larger numbers

Main activity

- Share the story, allow learners to respond freely then ask:
    - Why did the frog and snake do what they did?
    - What is the story's message?
    - What if other things were joined together like the snake and the frog?
- Share your prepared ideas, product success criteria and creativity focuses
- Ask learners for their own ideas, allowing time for individual reflection and paired/group discussion

- Suggest further creative starting points – objects, colours, plants, places, machines, and so on
- Respond to their ideas, then set a time limit for individuals, pairs or groups to create one or more products

Plenary

- Ask learners to check each other's products to see how well the criteria have been met
- Choose a sample of the products to share with the whole group
- Ask learners if they have been:
  - seeing things in a different way
  - making things that haven't existed before
- Record their comments publicly where they can be referred to easily
- Ask learners what they would like to create next

Support, extension and application

For younger or emerging creators:

- Work on making only 1 creative connection between 2 objects
- Physically connect real and familiar objects together in never-ending cycles – e.g. construction kits / modelling clay / material / children holding hands
- Create models, pictures or tableaux of the frog and the snake locked together

For older or more experienced creators:

- Connect more than 2 things in a never-ending cycle
- Make never-ending cycles, then challenge others to work out the connection to the learning/message
- Instead of cycles, create spirals of ideas where each new connection must in some way build on the previous one

Applications

Make never-ending cycles using the following as starting points:

Mathematics
- numbers, patterns and sequences

Language and communication
- words, sentences, stories, sign language, symbols

Science and technology
- processes, natural features – weather/tides

Art and design
- storyboards, colours, patterns, textures

Health and well-being
- exercise routines, courses of a meal

Human, social and environmental
- recycling processes, migration, dates, artefacts

The Reluctant Wizard

There was once a young wizard who lived alone in a hut amongst the moss and the stones and the trees of a deeply magical forest. Like most wizards, he wore his grey hair long and his beard was untrimmed. Like most wizards, he preferred dark flowing robes and he carried a staff to cast particularly large and interesting spells with. Like most wizards, he had parentage that was questionable.

As you well know, some wizards are born of people who shouldn't have given birth to them, others come from animals, and a few appear mysteriously during storms and snow showers. This wizard was unique amongst his kind because he had four parents – two mothers and two fathers. One set, a pair of wise old dwarfs, had raised him. The other, two lean young elves, had made him.

He didn't have much to do with any of them – in fact, he favoured his own company over that of others. And herein lay a tricky problem. You see, this wizard was very good at magic – in fact, he was the best in the land. Because of his skills, people would seek him out and ask him to cast spells for them. He always helped them – even if seventy-seven people called on him (as happened one day). And they did come, asking for healing and teaching and help with finding things and solving problems, and making all sorts of well-intentioned requests. But he always helped them slowly and with a glum face. He'd much rather be on his own making up new spells.

So he lived in constant conflict: he wanted to be alone, and he wanted to help, and he could only help if he wasn't alone. What made it worse was that his four parents kept calling on him, and what made it even worse was that the National Wizard Federation wanted him to work for them, and what made it even worse than that was the International Committee of Advanced Wizards wanted him to advise them. All by Sunday tea-time.

He was only young (107 years old), but all these demands were becoming too much for him. They gave him a pain in his chest and sometimes one in his shoulders too. So with his staff in his hand and a small box of provisions, he set off one day for his special thinking place.

After a day's walking he reached a quiet clearing. The sunlight fell like clear water on a mist of blue and yellow flowers. Animals rustled in the nearby bushes and colourful birds made music in the surrounding trees.

The wizard put down his staff, sat on his favourite thinking rock, closed his eyes and began to breathe deeply. After a while the clearing became silent. A purple light appeared all around the wizard and he began to smile. After a while longer the light faded and the noises came back. However, the smile stayed on the wizard's face.

He hopped off the rock, picked up his things and walked back to his hut (it took him considerably less time to return because a spring had appeared in his step).

When he woke the next day the smile was still there, and he greeted the people who called on him joyfully.

Let's create

Some creative ideas are the result of a process (see flash box, p. 22). Others just pop into our heads, often when we're least expecting them – maybe in the bath, while driving, running, cooking, meditating (like the reluctant wizard), walking home from the pub or taking a shower. Young children are brimming with questions and ideas. Sir Ken Robinson asked the question 'Do schools kill creativity?' in his now famous TED talk in June 2006. If there's the slightest risk of this, we have a duty to safeguard our learners' intuitive creativity by helping them to recognise, record and therefore value it. Here's a simple way to do just that.

Learners will create

A shower book in which appear all the interesting places and times at which they have their ideas, together with the fantastic ideas themselves.

Shower book:

❶ Can easily be carried around and to and from school

❷ Is durable enough to survive being carried about

❸ Has a personalised and named cover with at least:

- 4 colours
- 3 pictures
- 2 unexpected things

❹ Contains thoughts, ideas and the places/times when the thoughts/ideas happened

❺ Contains words, sketches, cuttings, found things, photos, diagrams and anything else that can be fixed in.

Learners will develop

A belief that creative potential is inside everyone and may be found everywhere

An ability to seek out new ideas and experiences actively

An attitude of openness to new ideas and experiences when they appear

An attitude of non-judgement

You will need

Your own shower book with several pages already filled in and an awareness of when and where ideas pop into your head

A selection of blank books suitable to become shower books and materials with which to personalise them – if book-making features in your planning, alter it to shower book-making

Main activity

- Share the story, allow learners to respond freely, then ask:
  - Why did the wizard struggle?
  - What happened at the wizard's thinking place?
  - What if ideas pop into heads at unexpected times?
- Ask learners what ideas they've had and when and where they've had them
- Look for common themes and record their ideas publicly
- Show your shower book and share when and where your own ideas come
- Share success criteria for a shower book and give learners time to personalise and prepare their own
- Ask learners to begin using their shower book and be prepared to share after a week or so

Plenary (after a week)

- Show learners what you've added to your own shower book during the week
- Ask learners to share their books with each other without judging or criticising
- Find out where and when learners have their ideas and what sort of ideas they have
- Ask learners if they:
  - found ideas just popping into their heads
  - found ideas in lots of different places
  - looked for ideas or waited for them to come
  - managed not to judge someone else's book
- Record their comments publicly where they can be referred to easily
- Ask learners how they might want to use their shower books from now on

Support, extension and application

For younger or emerging creators:

- Call it 'eye book' or a 'look book', in which learners record interesting things they've seen (consider ear book / sound book or hand book / touch book as well)
- Create a whole-class look book
- Allow learners to talk freely and at length about their ideas

For older or more experienced creators:

- Develop the shower book into a think book or a creative journal
- Create on-line shower books using Wikispaces or similar
- In pairs/groups look for themes and connections across different shower books

Applications

Shower books raise the profile of intuitive creativity. They are valuable as a creativity tool that bubbles away in the background of a creative learning environment.

They can also be customised and applied to specific curriculum content:

Mathematics
- Numbers, shapes, interesting uses of maths, problems

Language and communication
- Interesting words, symbols, sounds, conversations, questions

Science and technology
- Machines, changes, weathers, forces, big questions, experiments

Art and design
- Colours, textures, shapes, products, public art, reflections, shadows

Health and well-being
- Food and drink, sports, risks, emotions

Human, social and environmental
- People, buildings, dates, old photos, waste, beliefs

Arturo's Balloon

In the foot of his Christmas stocking Arturo found a balloon. Arturo loved balloons, so he forgot all about his other presents. Now, if you're very young (or very old), you'll know that blowing up balloons can be a tricky business: getting your lips to stay in the right place, putting your tongue where it should be, finding enough puff to start it off, and then keeping the air in it once you've managed all that. Arturo was only 6 and he puffed and blew until his cheeks were pink and his head went dizzy. But the balloon stayed small and floppy in his little hand.

He had another go and another and another, but the balloon just wouldn't inflate. So Arturo sat down in front of the Christmas tree. Suddenly he realised that something was not quite right. One of the Christmas tree decorations – a silver bauble – was far bigger than it ought to be. It was as big as a basketball and it was so heavy that the branch where it hung bent all the way down to the carpet. There was yet another strange thing. The remote control on top of the television was now the size of a loaf of bread, and each button was as big as a 10p piece. Then Arturo got an even bigger surprise: his left slipper was three times as long as it was supposed to be – just like a clown's shoe.

Arturo was quite scared at first, but curiosity got the better of him as he set about working out what had happened. And very soon he did. He brought the balloon back up to his mouth, faced towards the sofa, and then blew. What happened next proved that he was right! Although the balloon grew no bigger, the sofa expanded a little in time with each of his breaths. He kept blowing until the sofa was twice its normal size – so big that he would need to climb up on a chair to get on it.

Arturo had found a powerful magic balloon in his stocking! Whenever you tried to blow it up, whatever was in front of you got blown up instead. Without knowing, he'd already inflated a Christmas decoration, the remote control, his slipper and now the sofa.

Time for some fun, thought Arturo.

First (after taking off his big slipper) he tiptoed upstairs and blew up his sister's clarinet. That would stop her noisy practising – she wouldn't even be able to get it in her mouth! Then he went back downstairs to the kitchen and inflated the biscuit tin – and the biscuits inside were suddenly five times as big with five times as much chocolate on top. Next he went to his dad's study and blew the magic balloon at the door – that made the door so big that Dad wouldn't ever be able to open it to get inside again. And, finally, he poked his head out of the front door and blew up next door's cat. He gave the balloon ten extra puffs, and when he'd finished the cat was as tall as the houses in Arturo's street. The cat thumped off, squashing cars and destroying sheds.

That was great, thought Arturo, and he gave the balloon a huge blow in celebration. It was a pity that, just as he did so, he caught sight of himself in the hall mirror.

Let's create

One of the easiest ways to create something new is to begin with a familiar object and make one simple change to it. Arturo's balloon does this. But there are other straightforward changes that can take place to create interesting variations on a theme. Extra items can be added or removed; features enlarged, reduced or substituted; and objects reversed or multiplied.

Learners will create

A flash box that can be used to generate new ideas and objects from existing ones quickly. The box is nothing more than a small box (such as a shoebox) containing items that each represent a creative change. A balloon, for example, could represent enlargement.

The flash box needs to:

❶ be a small box holding up to 10 objects

❷ contain objects that represent simple changes

❸ be decorated with at least 3 things that sparkle, 3 that are furry and 3 that are natural (feel free to negotiate other features)

❹ include the words 'flash box'

Learners will develop

An ability to make, think or do things that haven't been made, thought or done before

An attitude of non-judgement

An ability to see familiar things in new and different ways

You will need

Several boxes suitable to become flash boxes, together with materials for decoration.

A selection of objects that represent ways in which features of an object can be altered:

- Enlargement, represented by a balloon
- Splitting up, represented by a jigsaw piece
- Removal, represented by a pair of tweezers
- Addition, represented by glue
- Combination, represented by a mixing spoon

Main activity (plus homework task over 2 days)

- Share the story, allow learners to respond freely, then ask:
  - What happened to Arturo at the end of the story?
  - What if the balloon didn't make things bigger, but did something else?
- Ask learners to discuss different ways in which things can change
- Ask them to make a list of changes, add some of your own, then get them to choose objects to represent each change
- Encourage learners to listen to the ideas in your list impartially
- Share success criteria and give learners time to make and fill their own – individually, in pairs or in small groups

Plenary (after homework)

- Present flash boxes to each other and describe their contents
- Try them out by applying different kinds of changes to objects and ideas (see applications below)
- Again encourage learners to listen to these ideas impartially
- Ask learners if they:
  - have made or thought about things that they've not made or thought about before
  - managed to not judge other people's ideas
  - have been able to see objects as representations of changes
- Record their comments publicly where they can be referred to easily
- Ask learners how they might use a flash box

Support, extension and application

For younger or emerging creators:

- Keep the changes simple and few in number
- Dedicate further time and resources to making the flash boxes
- Demonstrate changes with real objects

For older or more experienced creators:

- Suggest more complicated or multi-part changes
- Add items to the box that have no purpose yet
- Define different versions of the same change – e.g. 'enlarging' could include doubling, tripling or increasing one specific feature only

Applications

A flash box may be used to create new objects and ideas by applying simple changes to existing ones. It may kick-start creative thinking and deepen understanding of subject knowledge.

Apply flash box changes to these subjects:

Mathematics

- Shapes, numbers, sets of objects

Language and communication

- Fictional characters, lines from a poem, descriptive words, story plots

Science and technology

- Materials, natural phenomena

Art and design

- Famous paintings/sculptures, household objects, toys

Health and well-being

- Body systems, diets, game rules

Human, social and environmental

- Public buildings, historical events

A flash box may also be used to suggest creative solutions to problems or challenges – e.g. 'How can we have better playtimes?':

- Enlargement (balloon) – more time or space to play
- Splitting up (jigsaw piece) – different areas for different activities
- Removal (tweezers) – identify and remove the problems
- Addition (glue) – add structure, add music, add games
- Combination (mixing spoon) – mix in a learning area, combine playtime with school clubs

The Golden Steps

A young woman once decided to set out on a journey. She wanted to see distant lands and cross vast blue oceans. She wanted to meet exciting people: storytellers, jugglers, magicians, artists, scientists and musicians. She longed to taste exotic foods and spicy drinks. But most of all she hoped to find her fortune – a fortune of gold! So, with these dreams in her head and bread, cheese and water in her bag, she stepped on to the track outside her house and began to walk.

Before long she came upon a dusty flight of steps blocking the way. It stretched right across the road and rose up and up into the sky. As far as the clouds it reached. Well, the young woman hadn't expected her adventures to begin so soon, but there was nothing for it but to climb up the steps and see what was at the top. She put her foot on the first step. When she lifted it off, she saw that her boot had made a mark in the dust – a shiny mark. She stooped down and brushed more dust away. What do you know? The step was made of solid gold!

Well, not only had her journey been short, but she'd already found her fortune – all before lunchtime. Still, she was more than a little bit curious. If this staircase is made of solid gold, what riches must lie at the very top?, she thought.

After a quick lunch, she set off again. Up and up she went, higher and higher, each step a step of solid gold. She counted as she went – three, four, five … twenty-six, twenty-seven … one hundred and eighty-eight … With each step she felt richer and richer (she hadn't yet thought how she was going to get all this gold home), and as she felt richer and richer she felt greedier and greedier, and this made her steps faster and faster, which meant she got richer and richer quicker and quicker, and then the greed got bigger too (you get the idea).

By now, she was through the clouds and frantic to see what came next. Three hundred and thirty-one. She was convinced that some marvellous lost treasure must be sitting at the top of the steps and that it was a treasure she absolutely had to have. And then she saw that she was right – there, twinkling and shimmering in the bright sun, was a crown made of an enormous diamond, and it was studded with rubies, emeralds and sapphires. Faster and faster she ran, desperate to have the prize. Three hundred and sixty-seven, three hundred and sixty-eight … and then she was at the last step and …

Bang! She stopped. She didn't choose to stop; she just couldn't go any farther. She tried to take the last step, but for some reason she couldn't. She found her leg was back where it started. She tried again and the same thing happened. She tried with her other leg. It ended up where it started. She took three steps back and ran up, but as soon as she came to the last step, again she stopped. There was nothing in the way, she could reach past the step with her hand, but as soon as she tried to walk there, she froze.

Anger grew from a seed to a red spiky bush inside her faster than you could blink, and she kicked out at the last step. But as soon as she kicked, her foot came right back to where it had started. She kicked and kicked and kicked. Her rage was like a storm fighting a whirlwind. She kicked the step three hundred and sixty-seven times before she sat down and wept.

It was then that she looked behind her and saw that all but the last two steps had completely vanished.

Let's create

The activities in this section relate to 'The Golden Steps' and 'Ghramo's Mountain' (see pp. 24 and 108).

New things are created by combining chosen features of things that already exist. Here we shall combine 'The Golden Steps' and 'Ghramo's Mountain' into a brand-new tale. Each story has been distilled down to sixteen key elements that can be recombined in many different ways.

Learners will create

A story combining aspects of two other stories

Learners will develop

An ability to make, think or do things that haven't been made, thought or done before by them

A belief that creative potential is inside everyone and may be found everywhere

You will need

Copies of the sixteen pieces for each of the two stories (see pp. 120 and 121), scissors, Blu-Tack, glue

Main activity

- Share both stories over a couple of days, allow learners to respond freely, then ask,
  - What do the stories have in common?
  - Why do people want to climb?
  - What if the stories were combined?
- Show your learners the 16-piece distillation of each story
- Demonstrate how elements from each story may be combined to make the beginning of a new story
- Challenge learners to create a new story using some of the 32 pieces
- Cut out the pieces required and arrange them into the new story

Plenary

- Tell selected new stories
- Ask which features were used most often
- Ask learners if they:
  - made something new
  - realise that new things may be made by recombining existing ones
- Record their comments publicly where they can be referred to easily

Support, extension and application

For younger or emerging creators:

- Use familiar stories summarised in less than 16 pieces

- Change 1 feature – e.g. the main character

- Retell the new story for learners

For older or more experienced creators:

- Combine features from 3 or more stories

- Tell the new story in a different form – sounds, pictures, music, actions, dance, etc.

- Distill a short novel into 16 pieces

Applications

If two or more existing products/ideas are taken to pieces, then recombined into something new, learners can:

❶ discover more about the originals

❷ learn more about the theme by creating a new version

Here are several starting points to break down, then recombine:

Mathematics
- 2-tile patterns

Language and communication
- 2 poems

Science and technology
- 2 machines

Art and design
- 2 pieces of furniture

Health and well-being
- 2 sports

Human, social and environmental
- 2 buildings

Rain Fairies

When it rains, when it *really* rains, one million and four raindrops fall every second from each grey cloud in the sky. So every hour billions of raindrops fall down to Earth. One of them – one very special raindrop – has, trapped inside it, a rain fairy. If you are lucky enough to be outside and underneath the particular cloud from which that very special raindrop falls and if you haven't moved by the time it gets to you, then your luck might be in! The drop will splash on your head and the fairy will be free! But don't expect wishes or gifts or a tiny smiling servant to order about and do things for you. Oh no, expect something far more interesting than that.

In Denmark a rain fairy has just fallen on Rasmus. He's running home from school, away from the bullies. His satchel is swinging on his shoulder, his muddy shoes are splashing through the puddles, and his tears are mixing up with the rain on his face. Splash! A fairy is free! Rasmus stops. He knows that something amazing has happened but he can't yet tell what it is.

In India another fairy has popped open on Saraswati's head. She's waiting for her father to come home from the city. She misses him when he goes away. She's left all on her own. Sometimes he stays for a week and Saraswati goes hungry. But now her rain fairy is here. She feels something different, something wonderful.

In Scotland Douglas meets his fairy as he stands in line in the playground. They're picking teams again. He's last again. No one ever wants Douglas on their side. But his fairy is here now and something has changed. In Wales Glyndwr's fairy distracts him from his mother as she screams at him to hurry up and get in the car. In England Conway gets an incredible feeling inside as he trips and falls on to the pavement. And in Japan Natsuka sees something unbelievable when her sick old rabbit finally lays down its head and dies.

So, what is it about these rain fairies?

Let's create

'The Story' (p. 48) suggests that all stories follow a five-stage format. The final stage has been missed from the various threads of 'Rain Fairies'. We'll use a deceptively simple technique called the Glass Bead Game to explore the whole story and then come to some answers.

Learners will create

A Glass Bead Game that prompts them to explore unfinished events.

Learners will develop

An ability to use both analytic and holistic thinking

An ability to seek out new ideas and experiences actively

A belief that creativity can be a natural response to pain, suffering and boredom

You will need

Flipchart paper and pens, collections of small random objects

Main activity

- Share the story, allow learners to respond freely, then ask:
  - What do rain fairies do?
  - Why are there so few of them?
  - What if we knew exactly what happened to each of the children in the story?
- Arrange learners into groups of 4
- Explain the rules of the Glass Bead Game (see below):
  - choose a theme
  - take turns to play pieces associated with the theme
  - make creative links between pieces
  - devise a scoring system
  - discuss and evaluate the play
- Demonstrate how a game might be played around the theme of trees:

A point is scored for every piece played and every reasonable connection

Trees — Oak tree — **Oak**

Oak — Oak-wood kitchen — **Table**

Trees — Begin with 'T' — **Table**

Trees — Trees absorb — **CO$_2$**

CO$_2$ — A 'table' of CO$_2$ emissions — **Table**

Table — Dining table leaves for expansion — **Leaf**

- Ask groups to play the Glass Bead Game and explore what the rain fairies might be doing

Plenary

- Ask groups to explain how their game worked:
  - Did they manage to work out anything about the fairies?
  - How might the rules be changed to make the game better?
- Ask learners if they:
  - stuck to the rules
  - played unexpected pieces or made surprising connections
- Record their comments publicly where they can be referred to easily

Support, extension and application

For younger or emerging creators:

- Provide simple pieces related to the story and a template game board with fewer than 10 set places and connections
- Play the game on a big scale using cones and rope

For older or more experienced creators:

- Use small objects as pieces, making sure that each piece has a link to its meaning – e.g. a coin might mean wealth, a dice luck
- Join 2 or more games together

Applications

Glass Bead Games are inspired by the pastime hinted at in Herman Hesse's Nobel prize-winning novel of the same name.

This open-ended and customisable thinking process can be applied extensively in these areas:

Mathematics
- Numbers

Language and communication
- Adverbs

Science and technology
- Chemicals/elements

Art and design
- Textures

Health and well-being
- Body parts

Human, social and environmental
- Types of evidence

The Glass Bead Game

Choose a theme; all ideas must be linked to this. Choose a game board or create your own. Two to four players take turns to place/write ideas in empty spaces not currently connected to other ideas. As each new idea is placed, the player says how it is related to the others to which it is connected by a line. Continue until the board is complete, then summarise the thinking that's taken place. You could score 1 for every valid idea and 1 for every valid connection.

Foible Carrion's Curious Cabinet

Foible Carrion is the finest author in the land. Yet none of his work has ever been published: not a single book, story, poem or article. His style is clear and fluent, his topics witty and clever, his stories magical and engaging. But the world is not quite ready for him. So his words lay in sheaves, loose bound and falling to bits, locked in a cabinet in his study. Any number of publishers have rejected them with a curt word and a short note. Even so, Foible still spends his time writing at his desk. The magic still pours out, but he's the only one reading it.

If you were to stand in his study and peer into the cabinet, you might glimpse fragments like these:

One cold night a great storm blew over the Isle of Clouds, causing her to break free of her moorings and float out into the middle of the Irish Sea.

'Who's steering this thing?' shouted the islanders.

'No one. As usual,' shouted back the mayor.

Uncle Barry had escaped again. When we found him, he was stuck up a tree in Carnforth, clutching a big bag of meat pies. Anyone who walked under Uncle Barry's tree got one thrown at their head.

In a second-hand book shop next to the railway station, a man sits behind the counter all day, waiting for his wife to return. He has been sitting behind the counter for forty years. His wife, meanwhile, is standing in the next room, listening, waiting for him to come through with the tea.

Mr Lucas Hamster was unable to hold his skin up around his body for more than an hour at a time. It worked loose, puffed up, then began to sag in folds around his bones. It also changed colour each time it fell off. It was a tiresome process hooking it back on again.

There was once a land where disagreements were settled with the throw of three mystical dice. Children who fought each other in the playground used the dice, families who argued about money and time used the dice, businesses that stole each other's ideas used the dice, and politicians who argued in public used them too.

Under a small stone at the back of a cave, Remus discovered the greatest piece of knowledge the world would ever know. Everything was the same. Everything came from the same one thing. Therefore everything could become everything else. That was the secret. If only Remus could bring this knowledge into the world …

Rose Gravely's father did not consider child-mining to be a suitable career for his beloved daughter. But she was a determined young woman and, despite her father's intense and sometimes violent protests, found herself at the age of 26 manageress of the largest child mine in the world.

And then, one day, sad and unfulfilled and with a pen still in his hand, Foible Carrion stopped writing and died. No one came to his funeral and all his possessions were given away. The cabinet could not be unlocked, so it stands – papers and all – in the cellar of a junk shop in a northern town called Askrigg. If you can possibly get your hands on it, maybe you'd like to finish what Foible started.

Let's create

Locked inside Foible's cabinet are hundreds of unfinished writing projects. The obvious creative kick-start would be to pick a story opening and continue it. But creativity is not always about the obvious; it's about the unexpected.

Learners will create

A cabinet full of objects that can be used as starting points for creative thought and action.

The cabinet can be anything. However, it must:

❶ be labelled 'The Curious Cabinet of Creativity'

❷ allow for everything within it to be seen at the same time

❸ have enough separate spaces for each learner to display at least 1 item

❹ always have empty spaces

Each item in the cabinet must:

❶ be smaller than …

❷ be safe and harmless

❸ have permission from its owner for it to be in the cabinet

❹ be interesting or unfamiliar

❺ be able to remain in the curious cabinet until further notice

Learners will develop

A belief that creative potential is inside everyone and may be found everywhere

An ability to seek out new ideas and experiences actively

An attitude of smart risk-taking

You will need

An empty creative cabinet that meets the above criteria. Build it yourself or have your learners design and make one but don't tell them what it's for – create an air of mystery.

Possible cabinets:

- A display wall with individual taped- or ribboned-off areas
- Many shoeboxes pinned to a wall
- A real glass-fronted cabinet
- Many empty matchboxes

You'll also need a few objects for going into the cabinet.

Main activity (plus homework task over 2 days)

- Share the story, allow learners to respond freely, then ask:
  - Which story opening was the most curious?
  - What if we had a curious cabinet?
- Look at your cabinet
- Show your curious items and share criteria for discovering more
- Give learners 2 days to find an item to put in the cabinet
- Encourage them to take a smart risk and look in non-obvious places
- Remind them to think and keep safe when seeking an object

Plenary (after homework task)

- When all the objects have been placed in the cabinet, allow learners to talk to each other about what's in there
- Ask them for a question or a comment about any item

- Ask learners if they:
  - realise that objects could have come from anywhere
  - actively looked for something different
  - took a risk in what they chose
- Record their comments publicly where they can be referred to easily
- Ask learners how they might use the cabinet and its contents

Support, extension and application

For younger or emerging creators:

- Provide several objects; learners choose which to put in the cabinet
- Relax or adapt the item criteria
- Use fewer than 10 items

For older or more experienced creators:

- Enhance the item criteria – e.g. the item must be unfamiliar to everyone in the class, the item must be linked to a particular theme (see below)
- Add 1 or more extra layers to the cabinet to create spaces in which to hide items
- Items must be placed next to others with which a reasoned connection can be made

Applications

A curious cabinet of creativity, full of interesting items, has many uses:

- Objects or combinations of objects may be used to stimulate creative expression. For example:
  - choose any 3 objects and create a story/dance/song/collage that includes them
  - describe 1 of the objects without naming it while others guess which it is
- Seeking connections and relationships between objects stimulates creative thinking – e.g.:
  - find a connection between 3 adjacent objects
  - decide which of 5 objects could be the odd 1 out
  - find a connection between a new object and 4 that are already in the cabinet

A cabinet may be customised to specific knowledge content. For example:

Mathematics

- Put in numbers and symbols and seek connections and patterns between adjacent items

Language and communication

- Put in interesting words and create novel sentences

Science and technology

- Put in different materials and seek common features

Art and design

- Put in works of art (or reduced copies) as a themed gallery

Health and well-being

- Put in sports-related items and information, and seek connections or create new activities

Human, social and environmental

- Put in historical artefacts and build alternative histories

Tanoma and the Snake

Tanoma loved to be by himself and he loved to be outside. But the other members of his tribe did not approve because each person was supposed to be part of the community, living and working together. As a boy Tanoma had always hated having to play with the other children, and even now he couldn't bear being with his family in their small log house. So he spent his days walking alone in the forest, enjoying the solitude.

Over the years he had learned the names of all the trees and flowers. He understood the behaviour of the birds and animals and recognised each one by its call. He had discovered hidden pathways that criss-crossed the woodland and he could identify all the coloured bugs and spiders that lurked under stones and in decaying logs. In all this time Tanoma had thought that he was alone, but he was mistaken. Amonat, an evil witch, lived in a twisted old tree in the heart of the forest. She'd often watched Tanoma on his walks, spying from behind a rock or from within a hole in the ground.

One day she decided to test him. She turned herself into a young woman and sat down in a clearing between the trees. She made sure that she was near a path that Tanoma was certain to take. She set a bowl made from bark on her knees and, sure enough, before the sun reached its highest point in the sky, he appeared.

When Tanoma saw what looked like a beautiful young woman, he stopped and quickly darted behind a tree. As he watched, he saw the woman catch a snake and drop it into the bowl. Then she began to sing quietly. After a time she poured in some water and continued her singing. At last she stopped singing and picked up several small sticks. She dropped them into the bowl as well and, all of a sudden, the sticks sprang to life and began dancing about, eventually hopping right out of the bowl and scurrying off into the undergrowth. After this the young woman closed her eyes and drifted off into a trance. The snake curled around itself and settled down to sleep.

Tanoma had never seen anything like it. He waited until darkness fell before creeping out from behind the tree and slowly approaching the woman. Ever so carefully he reached towards her and, without disturbing the sleeping snake, gently lifted the bowl from her knees. He checked that she was still in her trance, then walked silently into the forest.

When he was far away, he sat down and put the bowl on his own knees. He grabbed a handful of grass and dropped it in. Immediately the blades came to life and scuttled off into the night. He experimented with stones and earth and flowers and berries, and each time the things awoke and jumped out of the bowl. Tanoma wondered what use he could make of such powerful magic.

The next day he caught another snake and placed it in the bowl. He poured in a little more water, and as he did so the first snake woke up, flicked its tail and sent some drops right into his eyes. When Tanoma opened them, he was astonished to find that he could see through the trees to the village and mountains beyond. When he looked down, he saw the roots of the trees and all the creatures that lived under the ground. And looking up, through the clouds, he could make out the glimmer of distant stars that were not normally visible in the day. As the water was replaced by moisture from his own eyes the magic faded, but it left him eager to put another snake in the bowl.

This he quickly did and, without a single thought about what might happen, he brought the bowl to his lips, and carefully took a tiny sip of the liquid …

Let's create

Through an accidental 'spill of magic', Tanoma's eyes come alive and he is able to see the world differently. This hints at a valuable aspect of creativity – the ability to observe people, objects and events in new and interesting ways. A metaphor for this type of viewing is looking through a special pair of glasses – for example, rose-tinted glasses allow only the good things to pass through. In this activity children will create their own unique set of creative spectacles.

During this activity be sensitive to children in your class who wear spectacles. You could replace 'spectacles' with 'monocle' or 'pince-nez'.

Learners will create

1 or more pairs of creative glasses to contribute to the class spec bank. Each pair must:

- Clearly indicate what it allows the wearer to see
- Be decorated in some way that links to its purpose

Learners will develop

An ability to see familiar things in new and different ways

A belief that creative potential is inside everyone and may be found everywhere

An attitude of openness to new ideas and experiences when they appear

You will need

Card templates of a pair of spectacle frames such as the one shown below:

Main activity

- Share the story, allow learners to respond freely, then ask:
  - What was Tanoma able to see after the liquid got in his eyes?
  - Why did the witch decide to test Tanoma?
  - What if Tanoma became able to see in different ways?
- Make sure that your learners realise that Tanoma was able to see through things and far into the distance
- Explain the concept of rose-tinted spectacles and suggest other tints – e.g. spectacles that see only:
  - green things or plastic things or things with moving parts
  - sounds or thoughts or feelings or dreams
  - numbers or patterns or living things or forces
- Ask learners to think up some spectacles of their own and then take a blank pair and create them with the help of the template above

Plenary

- Share spectacles and practise using them in different parts of the school and outside

- Decide on a place in the classroom where the spectacles can be stored

- Ask learners if they:

  - have learned to see familiar things in different ways

  - believe that new ideas may be found all over the place

  - were willing to use the spectacles

- Record their comments publicly somewhere they can be referred to easily

Support, extension and application

For younger or emerging creators:

- Play with spectacles that have coloured plastic lenses that show the world in red/green/blue, etc.

- Create spectacles that focus on familiar and concrete features such as people, shapes, furniture

- Introduce 1 new set of spectacles at a time

For older or more experienced creators:

- Look through 2 or more sets of spectacles simultaneously – filtering by 2 or more criteria

- Create complex and abstract spectacles such as ones that see 10 seconds into the future or that see people's beliefs

- Have someone describe what they see through a pair of spectacles and work out what the spectacles do

Applications:

Single pairs of creative specs can be used to focus on specific learning points – e.g. specs that see only adjectives help to boost creative writing; specs that see only forces support scientific understanding. The classroom spec bank may be used freely when new ideas are needed and when different points of view must be taken into account. Here are a few ideas for creative specs that see only:

Mathematics
- Right angles

Language and communication
- Pauses in talking

Science and technology
- Liquids

Art and design
- Shadow

Health and well-being
- Things that move on their own

Human, social and environmental
- Recyclable things

The Town called Est

The beautiful town of Est was built on an island in the sea. The currents around the island were unpredictable and deadly, and the tide came in and out at the speed of a galloping horse. Hundreds of unlucky travellers had met a watery death as the tide unexpectedly rose up around them.

Est was surrounded by a high wall into which was set an enormous wooden gate. This gate allowed the citizens to reach the mainland when the tide was low, and held back the water when the tide was especially high. If the gate were ever to be left open at high tide, Est would be flooded and many people would perish. So the gate was closed in good time each day. The King locked it personally with a golden key that never left a chain hung around his neck.

One summer's day Dellan, the King's daughter, was strolling through the streets of Est when she met a man. He was a stranger to her, so she introduced herself. He replied, eager to talk to someone. They talked and strolled together, and before long they had become friends. By the time daylight fell and her father was closing the gate at the other side of the town, she realised that she had fallen in love with this man and wanted to spend a lot more time with him.

Unfortunately Dellan was utterly unsuspecting of this man's true nature. He was really a charming and extremely well-disguised demon.

Dellan begged him to meet her again and he agreed. They spent the following day together and the next, and by the end of a week Dellan was so in love that she would have done anything for him. The demon could sense this, so he asked her to get for him her father's golden key. At first she said no, but he was very persuasive. He claimed that by having the key he would take the great burden of protecting Est from her father's shoulders. He persuaded her that the key was at risk of being stolen and needed a safer home. He said that if Dellan really did love him, then surely she would do this small thing for him.

So Dellan agreed, and that night she crept into her father's bedchamber and unhooked the key from the chain around his neck. She returned to the man she loved and handed the key to him. Only then did he reveal his true identity, and Dellan was distraught. The demon ran off and unlocked the gate. The tide was on its way in, but everyone in Est was sound asleep and they all believed they were safe from the rising water.

The demon leaped on to a horse and sped off out of the gate. The water was low enough to let him through, but its level was climbing quickly and soon the town would be not only cut off but flooded.

Dellan cleared her head, wiped her tears and felt utter fury at how she had been tricked. She woke her father and told him everything. They both jumped on to the town's fastest horse and set off, the angry King in front and Dellan clinging on behind him. The water was rising fast. The demon heard his pursuers, looked back over his shoulder and laughed. This angered the King even more, and he spurred on the horse. He was determined to catch the thief who had tricked his daughter and was about to destroy his town. The water came higher and both horses slowed as they found it harder and harder to run through the sea.

And then a voice came into the King's head. It told him that the only way to catch the demon, retrieve the key and save the city was to let Dellan slide off to her death in the sea. That was his choice. Dellan or his people. The demon knew this too and he laughed even louder.

So the King made the only choice a true king could. He told Dellan exactly what she must do to save the town, leaped off the horse and was swallowed up by the unpredictable and deadly waters.

Let's create

This story is based on a Breton fairy tale about the town of Is. Dellan and her father are forced into a tragic finale because she failed to see through the demon's disguise. He was able to conceal his true nature from her.

Masks endow us with a powerful means of expression and a great deal of self-confidence. We can hide behind them and do things that we wouldn't do if our faces were exposed. Masks may help young learners to understand themselves, develop their personalities and build up their confidence when performing in front of others.

Learners will create

A 2-face that expresses a hidden personality

Learners will develop

An ability to make, think or do things that haven't been made, thought or done before

You will need

Blank card, scissors and coloured pens

Main activity

- Share the story, allow learners to respond freely, then ask:
  - What did the demon want?
  - Why did Dellan fall for the demon?
  - What if the King had not jumped off the horse?
- Explain that Dellan's lover was not who he first appeared to be – he had a hidden, evil personality
- Quickly sketch a kind face and a devil's face on either side of a face-shaped piece of card, to represent the man's 2 natures
- Ask learners to pick 2 different personalities from:
  - happy, evil, sad, devious, old, young, bitter, kind, male, female (and others that learners suggest)
- Ask learners to create a 2-face card mask, each side of which shows a face with a different personality

Plenary

- Cut eye-holes, hold 2-faces up to real faces and act/speak in the personality of the face
- Reverse the face and change speech/actions to reflect the different nature
- Ask learners if they:
  - have created something new and of value to them
- Record their comments publicly where they can be referred to easily

Support, extension and application

For younger or emerging creators:

- Focus on simple personalities – happy/sad

- Group similar personalities together to talk to each other

- Associate colours with different personalities – e.g. angry has a red face

For older or more experienced creators:

- Create 2-faces with mixed personalities

- Debate important issues while assuming the 2-face personalities

- One learner argues a point from both personalities on their 2-face

Applications

Use a 'I agree / I don't agree' 2-face to debate key issues in different subjects

Thinking Fairy saves the Day

A man, a wolf, a goat and a cabbage stood at the edge of a river, waiting to cross. There was one small boat and only two of them could get in it at the same time. What's more, if they were left alone without the man the goat would eat the cabbage and the wolf would eat the goat. The man had to keep everything in order. It was a real puzzle.

They tried a few combinations but the cabbage got nibbled, the goat got a nasty bite and the wolf received a jolly good telling-off from the man. They all sat down and sighed.

'I'm sick of being in this story,' said the goat. 'All day long I have to stay here with you lot by this river, while our readers try to figure out how we can get across.'

'Me too,' said the wolf, 'I'm tired of going backwards and forwards in that boat and biting your leg whenever the people reading this story forget we can't share a ride.'

'Shh,' said the man. 'Although this is a story, you're not supposed to be able to talk. It's a problem, not a fable.'

'   ,' said the cabbage, because although the other characters were breaking the rules it, sadly, was still only a cabbage. And whoever heard of a talking cabbage?

'What we need,' said the wolf, 'is something more interesting to think about.' And right on cue the Thinking Fairy appeared.

'What you lot need,' advised the Thinking Fairy, 'is something more interesting to think about. So I shall grant you the gift of making up strange yet interesting problems.'

'Thank you, Thinking Fairy,' they all said (except the cabbage). And here's how it went.

The man got to choose a difficult journey – different from crossing a river. The wolf got to choose who or what went on the journey. The goat had to choose three different things to help on the journey. And the cabbage got to sit there and watch.

Here's the first problem they made:

How can we send a bottle of milk over the mountains using a tool, a small animal and a surprise?

'That's the idea,' laughed the fairy. 'Have another go.'

OK, then:

How can we transport a bag of money through a rabbit warren using a musical instrument, a vegetable and a loud noise?

'Spot on. Some of the best I've heard this week,' praised the fairy. 'Let's have one more before I slip back to fairyland.'

So man, wolf, goat and cabbage sat on the river bank for the rest of the day inventing weird and wacky problems. And when it was time to go home, no one had eaten anyone else, everyone agreed it had been a most enjoyable day, and of course they'd completely forgotten why they wanted to cross the river in the first place.

Let's create

At some time in our lives we are likely to be presented with a classic logic problem like the one that begins this story. This version provides a humorous launchpad for creating weird, wacky and crazy challenges that will help your learners to develop problem-solving skills for use in more serious situations.

Learners will create

Crazy challenges prompted by a table of weird ideas, together with equally wacky solutions.

Learners will develop

A belief that creativity can change things and improve things

A belief that creativity can be a natural response to pain, suffering and boredom

An ability to make, think or do things that haven't been made, thought or done before

You will need

Copies of the Crazy Challenge Table (p. 122)

Main activity

- Share the first 2 paragraphs of the story, then ask:
  - What should they do to cross the river safely?
  - Why do they want to cross the river?
  - What if they could all talk? What would they say?
- Share the rest of the story and ask for ideas to solve one or more of the new problems creatively
- Introduce and demonstrate the Crazy Challenge Table and ask learners to create 1 or more challenges
- Encourage learners to solve each other's challenges

Plenary

- Share several challenges and their solutions
- Value surprising, humorous, weird, clever and original ideas
- Ask learners if they:
  - made up new and interesting problems
  - have got better at solving problems
- Record their comments publicly where they can be referred to easily

Support, extension and application

For younger or emerging creators:

- Act out the original story with real animals (you can use a stuffed wolf if a real one is not easily to hand – same with the goat)

- Share interesting problems that you've faced and those in well-known fairy tales (e.g. Rapunzel's imprisonment)

- Demonstrate a new crazy challenge by acting it out

For older or more experienced creators:

- Increase the complexity of the challenge by picking more than 1 item from each column of the table

- Generate a new table by collecting features from real-life problems or problems presented in film/TV/literature

- Take a crazy solution and work back to a different crazy challenge that might have created that solution

Applications

Once learners have got to grips with the basics of any subject area, they will be ready to solve problems in that domain. A crazy challenge table helps to generate many new problems. Here are some suggestions for table headings for different subjects. You and your learners can fill in the columns and then create and solve the new challenges:

Mathematics – create number problems

- Items in a shop

- Prices

- Number of items

Language and communication – create story starters

- Good story characters

- Evil influences

- Quest to find a …

Science and technology – do everyday jobs in new ways

- Jobs around the house

- Tools

- Materials

Art and design – create artwork in different styles

- In the style of … (artists)

- Media

- Subjects of the artwork

Health and well-being – create new sports

- Sports equipment

- Number of players

- Pitches

Human, social and environmental – create new ways to travel

- Reason for journey

- Method of transport

- Entertainment

The Story

Once upon a time there lived a woman called Josephine Booker. She was a troubled woman because she had set herself a difficult task. Josephine had decided to collect every story in the world, and she knew she would not be content until she had done so. She had already filled several notebooks with stories, which amounted to about 793,000 pages. However, Josephine's undertaking was doomed to fail as no sooner had she written down one story than another three were made up. She might travel halfway round the Earth to sit for several hours inside the hut of a wise old man, waiting to hear him tell 'The Eagle who couldn't Fly' or 'The Horses of Tricky Wood', only to return home and discover that a book of twenty-seven new fairy tales had been published in Keswycke.

Josephine Booker had been gathering stories for thirty-four years. – thirty-four years of frustration and disappointment, and she was ready to give up. It was like trying to catch eels in a net made of a mesh with holes that were too big. She had become a discontented and bitter woman, and any hope of finishing her quest had all but vanished, but then Josephine heard something that restored her optimism. She heard about the Story.

Josephine decided to try to find The Story. She decided this would be her final journey. So we find her on a dusty road in Persia, striding purposefully towards the city of Chereh, where she believes the Story is hidden.

Travellers speak of the Story in hushed voices. Books hint at its existence but never reveal its true nature. Maps are vague and ambiguous about its location. However, Josephine thinks she knows where to find it. Since first hearing about the Story, she's spoken to many travellers, searched thousands of books and pored over numerous maps. If anyone can find the Story, Josephine can.

And now Josephine has arrived in the glittering city of Chereh. She is walking slowly up and down each of its streets trying to find the Story. She is going in and out of Chereh's public buildings – temples, libraries, palaces, shops – looking for the Story. She is talking in a hushed voice to travellers in dimly-lit bars asking questions about the Story.

The Sultan of Persia is informed that a strange woman has arrived in Chereh and is asking dangerous questions. So he sends his guards to find her. They discover her digging behind a statue in the main square and arrest her. Josephine is very angry. She thought the Story was hidden underneath the statue. She was so close.

The Sultan demands to know what Josephine is doing. When she tells him, he smiles a smile that has nothing to do with being happy and sends her to his dungeons. Josephine is locked away and given very little food. She must have offended the Sultan when she mentioned the Story. She saw his frown but she also saw fear in his eyes. Josephine gets weaker and weaker in her cell but her determination to find the Story keeps her alive.

One night she tells a guard about her quest and he is impressed that someone is so dedicated to doing one thing in life. The next night he doesn't lock Josephine's cell door and pretends to be asleep as she creeps out in to the moonlight. She returns to the statue in the main square and starts to dig again. She uses her bare hands and digs deeper and deeper until the hole is big enough for her to stand in and not be seen. Josephine finds a small door at the bottom of the hole at the base of the statue. She pushes the door open and there it is covered in cobwebs and dust: the Story. Josephine carefully reaches in and lifts it out like a newborn baby. Here it is – the end of her travels, the final stage, the end of the quest. Josephine can return home and die as a satisfied woman.

She looks at the Story and smiles and smiles and smiles, and then … and then her joy turns slowly to confusion and then fear as it dawns on Josephine that the Story isn't only the end to her quest. It is something much worse. The Story is every story. That's why Josephine wanted it – one story that sets the shape of all the others. Instead of finding every story, she needed to find this one only as all the others follow its form. The Story says how things are but as soon as you know it you are trapped inside it, just as Josephine has become. You will always know what comes next, how things will turn out, and life will become grey and pointless. Why do anything when you know how the story ends?

Josephine sits there frightened and covered in sand holding the Story and wondering, wondering, wondering if she should tell it.

Let's create

Many scholars have analysed the world's stories and claim to have found one pattern that underpins them all. In *The Seven Basic Plots* (Continuum 2004) Christopher Booker does just this and provides tons of evidence and a rather convincing argument. He says that the standard format goes something like this:

- A situation occurs where there is tension and something needs to be resolved
- A character is motivated to set out and resolve the tension
- Something makes the situation worse
- Something else counters this
- The 'somethings' in 3 and 4 engage and there is an outcome

That seems too simple, yet if you reflect on any well-known story, you will usually be able to pick out these five features.

Learners will create

A story inspection that analyses well-known stories for a single hidden pattern

Learners will develop

An ability to use both analytic and holistic thinking

An attitude of non-judgement

You will need

Copies of 'The Story' and access to a range of very short stories

A Story Inspection Sheet including:

- Does the story have:
- A problem to be sorted out?
- A character who sets out to solve the problem?
- The problem getting worse?
- An event or character trying to help?
- A struggle that ends in a solution or another problem?

Main activity

- Share the story, allow learners to respond freely, then ask:
  - What had Josephine found?
  - Why was she frightened?
  - What if she told the world her secret?

- Suggest to your learners that there is an ultimate story that is the template for all others. It has 5 stages:
  - there is a problem
  - a character sets out to solve the problem
  - the problem gets worse
  - an event or character tries to help
  - there is a struggle that results in a solution or another problem

- Provide blank Story Inspection Sheets and a range of very short stories.

- Ask your learners to inspect some stories to find out if they have the 5 stages

Plenary

- Ask learners to summarise their story and explain if and how the 5 stages appear in it.
- Do they think all the stories follow the same pattern?
- Ask learners if they:
  - used the inspection sheets correctly
  - were judging the stories or simply describing them
  - can think about the difference between judging and describing
- Record their comments publicly where they can be referred to easily

Support, extension and application

For younger or emerging creators:

- Look for 1 feature at a time – e.g. problems or good characters
- Inspect stories that are relevant and lived by learners – e.g. a story of going on holiday
- Use very familiar stories

For older or more experienced creators:

- Identify stories in popular fiction/film that either do not follow the 5-stage pattern or have the stages in a different order
- Create a possible new story pattern and write a story around it
- What happens to a story if 1 or more of the stages is missed out?

Applications

Inspection is necessary but not nearly sufficient to achieve high quality in learning. The skills of checking that a particular product has certain features are important, but the process by which it is made is equally valuable.

Learners can make their own checklist as a way to monitor the quality of their work and learning – checklists can apply to final products and processes. Here are examples of checklists for different subject areas:

Mathematics
- Features of 2D shapes

Language and communication
- Observable features of good listening

Science and technology
- A fair test

Art and design
- Customers' needs

Health and well-being
- A healthy lifestyle

Human, social and environmental
- An ethical choice

Jeremy Spaniel's Golden Thoughts

Jeremy Spaniel never goes out. He sits alone all day in his small bare room at the top of a grey stone house in a street called Melancholy Lane. In his room Jeremy has collected a few basic things: a wooden bed covered by a single white sheet, a brown plastic chair, a metal table with a wobbly leg and seven cloth-bound books, arranged on a shelf by the window.

The window overlooks next door's garden, around which a dog sometimes sniffs and in which children sometimes come to play. Jeremy spends some of his time looking out of this window and some of his time looking at his table. Every now and again he takes one of his books down from the shelf and reads a page or two. At 8 o'clock every evening bread, fruit and wine are left outside his door. When he hears them arrive, Jeremy waits for twenty minutes, then opens the door, picks them up and brings them inside. As the day ends he lights a small candle, eats his meal and then goes to bed. Every day is like this for Jeremy.

But one day Jeremy heard unexpected noises outside his door, an hour early. Strange footsteps were followed by an insistent rapping. Jeremy pretended that this wasn't happening and continued to stare at his table. But the knocking persisted and eventually he stood up, walked over to the door and opened it. A small man dressed in a black suit and carrying a briefcase pushed by him and sat right down on Jeremy's bed.

'Mr Spaniel,' he said in a precise and squeaky voice, 'we, of the Company, have reason to believe that your head is full of golden thoughts. We, of the Company, have watched you through your window. You do nothing and you go nowhere, so all this time your mind has had nothing to do but think. It's thought far more things than anyone else alive and has created thoughts that no one else has ever had. We, of the Company, are prepared to offer you exactly one hundred pieces of money in exchange for all of your golden thoughts. Sign here, please.'

'Hmm, golden thoughts, golden thoughts,' replied Jeremy dreamily as he signed the document that the little man held up to his face.

'Thank you, Mr Spaniel,' squeaked the man, who then reached inside his briefcase and pulled out a strange brass instrument that he pressed on to Jeremy's forehead …

Jeremy Spaniel is always going out now. He has many, many friends and is known throughout this city and the next. His conversation is witty and he is sought out by princes and princesses. Rarely can he be found at home in Melancholy Lane. He attends parties in trendy restaurants, visits famous writers and artists in their parlours, and may be seen shopping in the most expensive department stores. On rare occasions he ventures home to his room. Jeremy has collected there many frivolous things: a bed carved from the tallest redwood tree in Canada and covered with a duvet embroidered with silver threads, a jewelled throne bought from a king, a round table with seven sturdy legs, and a whole library of amusing and informative books that he never reads arranged on a case by the window.

Once in a while Jeremy glances through the window and looks down on to next door's garden. There he might spy a dog sniffing around or children playing, and in Jeremy's mind something stirs from an earlier time. He sees a ghost of himself slowly taking down one of the books from a shelf and reading a page or two. He tastes bread and fruit and wine, sees a flickering candle in a bare room and hears the echo of footsteps. And then in a moment these phantoms of memory are gone. Jeremy smiles and steps back into the glittering, golden city.

Let's create

This story leaves a lot of questions unanswered. What thoughts were in Jeremy's head? What did 'the Company' do with his thoughts? What remained in his head and how come he goes out more now? Why was he bored in the first place? What if he remembered his past life?

Oliver Postman once said, 'Children start school as question marks and leave as full stops.' Surely that's justification enough for keeping their questioning skills alive and thriving? The following activity provides a structured yet creative way to deepen and extend your pupils' questioning abilities.

Learners will create

A Chevalier board – stimulated and inspired by an interactive questioning activity at York Art Gallery, designed by author Tracy Chevalier – that prompts learners for a variety of questions about the story

Learners will develop

An ability to use both analytic and holistic thinking

An attitude of non-judgement

A belief that creativity can be a natural response to pain, suffering and boredom

You will need

Flipchart paper and pens

Copies of the Chevalier Board (see p. 123)

Main activity

- Share the story, allow learners to respond freely, then ask:
  - What questions do you have about the story?
  - Why does the story make you think of questions?
  - What if Jeremy were sitting with us in this room? What would you ask him?
- Arrange learners in groups of 4
- Provide a blank Chevalier board for each group (or ask learners to set out their own)
- Give groups a set time to generate the 4 types of question and write them in the 4 spaces (they may write as many as they like around the central prompt); questions must begin with:
  - What?
  - What if?
  - Why?

or they can be wild: any other question

- Ask groups to exchange boards and respond to the questions, but without directly answering the questions; they may write comments, ideas or further questions around the edge of the board
- Ask groups to pass the boards back

Plenary

- Ask groups to select their best question and the best response that they received from the other group (the response can be to a different question)
- Think about the challenges of the activity and how it might be altered

- Ask learners:
  - if they made appropriate responses to another group's questions
  - which type of questions are easiest to create
  - whether Jeremy was bored or creative, both or neither
- Record their comments publicly where they can be referred to easily

Support, extension and application

For younger or emerging creators:

- Develop the notion of 'a question' by:
  - explicitly modelling the use of different types of question
  - changing children's statements into questions
  - noticing, drawing attention to, recording publicly and celebrating children's own questions
- Remove the requirement for questions to begin with the 3 prompts
- Start by generating questions about familiar objects, people and situations

For older or more experienced creators:

- Pass Chevalier boards on to a third group so they can respond to the second group's responses
- Change the question prompts – e.g. questions beginning When, or How or What happens when …
- Evaluate questions and responses against agreed criteria

Applications

As long as answers are banned, a Chevalier board keeps the thinking process going. There may be times when you choose to allow answers and that's fine, but if you want your learners to drill down deep into their thinking, stick to the format above. The board may be used to open up thinking about a new topic and then to assess it at the end. Here are a few suggestions of themes for the central prompt:

Mathematics
- Mathematics in daily life – e.g. flight departure board

Language and communication
- Well-known fairy tales – e.g. 'Three Billy Goats Gruff'

Science and technology
- Household electrical devices – e.g. microwave

Art and design
- Works of art – e.g. Girl with the Pearl Earring

Health and well-being
- Common life events – a wedding

Human, social and environmental
- Places and people – e.g. a busy city street

The Boy who asked

There was once a boy called Reuben who worried because he did not know who he was. This troubled him day and night. He asked his parents.

'Well now, you're called Reuben and you're our beloved son, of course!' they said. But he was not satisfied with that.

He spoke to his friends. 'You are the fastest runner and the best tree climber we know,' they replied. But Reuben was not satisfied with that.

At school he asked his teacher. She explained, 'You are a thinker, an artist, a writer and the best tree climber I know.' But he was not satisfied with that either.

'*Who* am I?' he kept asking. 'Who *am* I?' He decided to look for the answer in other places. He packed some food in a tin and set off down the road.

Soon he met an old man coming the other way. 'Excuse me, sir, can you tell me who I am?'

The old man looked Reuben in the eye, then replied, 'No, I don't know who you are, but I see a handful of my wisdom inside you.'

Farther along the road he met an angel. 'Excuse me, angel, can you tell me who I am?'

The angel raised its wings and floated smoothly once around the boy. 'I cannot tell, but I sense a cupful of my goodness inside you.'

He walked on, and presently became aware of a devil hovering just behind him. Without stopping or turning, he asked, 'Excuse me, do you know who I am?'

'No,' breathed the devil, 'but my evil runs colder at the sight of you. You scare even me.'

Reuben was not satisfied with any of these answers. He sat down under a tree, opened his tin and began to eat. After a while a soldier came to sit beside him. He offered the soldier some of his food, then asked his question again.

The soldier closed his eyes, then said, 'I once asked myself the same question. I left my home many years ago and have been seeking the answer ever since. I have defeated the greedy and defended the weak. I have protected the greedy and overpowered the weak. Some people call me a hero; others think I'm a traitor. I have watched my friends die and my enemies live on. I have been left for dead in the battlefield mud and have recovered my health in the beds of golden palaces. I have loved and lost and cried and laughed till tears ran down my face. But after all of this, I still have no idea who I am.'

The soldier thanked Reuben for sharing his food, then continued on his way.

'*Who* am I? Who *am* I?' Reuben whispered. He knew that wisdom and goodness and evil were part of the answer. He knew he could climb trees, he knew he was loved, and he knew from the soldier that this was a very difficult question to answer. Reuben looked down into the empty tin.

A tear of frustration fell from his eye and splashed on to the shining metal. He looked at his face reflected there, then began to smile. An idea glinted in his mind. He looked a little closer – into the tin and into his thoughts – and there, at last, was an answer.

He had been carrying it with him all along. He now knew exactly who he was.

'I am the boy who asks, "Who am I?" I am the boy who loves to know.' He smiled. He was satisfied with that. For now.

Let's create

Reuben, the main character in this story, searches for and eventually discovers his identity. He is the boy who loves to know. He asks questions. He is driven to find out things, not least who he is.

The Chevalier Board (p. 123) generates questions in four categories. Here we widen the scope with a series of prompts and the challenge to create 101 questions.

Learners will create

101 questions about the story

Learners will develop

A belief that creative potential is inside everyone and may be found everywhere

An attitude of openness to new ideas and experiences when they appear

An ability to make, think or do things that haven't been made, thought or done before

You will need

Copies of How to Create 101 Interesting Questions (see p. 124) and a few interesting questions of your own about the story

Main activity

- Share the story, allow learners to respond freely, then ask:
  - What made the boy want to find out who he was?
  - Why couldn't the people he met on his journey answer his question?
  - What if no one knew who they were?

- Ask learners to think up 1 or 2 interesting questions about the story
- Share some of your own questions
- Introduce the prompt sheet and show how each starting point can stimulate a series of new questions
- Work through some examples – e.g. using the prompt of senses: touch
- Challenge individuals, pairs or small groups to generate 101 questions about the story

Plenary

- Ask learners to report back on how many questions they generated
- Ask learners to choose their best 3 questions

Ask learners if they:

- created unexpected questions that they'd not thought of before
- accepted all questions

- Record their comments publicly where they can be referred to easily

Support, extension, and application

For younger or emerging creators:

- Develop the notion of a 'question' by:
  - explicitly modelling the use of different types of question
  - changing children's statements into questions
  - noticing, drawing attention to, recording publicly and celebrating children's own questions
- Select age-/ability-appropriate prompts
- Start by generating questions about familiar objects, people and situations

For older or more experienced creators:

- Challenge them to generate additional prompts
- Ask them to create a set of 10 top questions that are most useful for learning about a new situation
- Work backward from generated questions to hidden prompts

Applications

'If you want to have one good idea, have 100 ideas first.' Quantity inevitably breeds quality. If learners generate 101 questions, they have more chance of hitting on three or four superb ones. The ability to ask an extensive range of questions allows them to explore any topic to deeper and wider levels. Here are a few starting points for using the 101 questions prompt sheets:

Mathematics
- A tessellating pattern

Language and communication
- A book cover

Science and technology
- A fair test and its results

Art and design
- A piece of public art

Health and well-being
- A sport

Human, social and environmental
- A historical event

The Hidden Gift

One day an old man stepped out of the forest. His back was bent and he shuffled along the path, wheezing and coughing. His tired face was lined and dirty and his clothes were worn and full of holes. All in all, he was not a pretty sight. People peeped at him through the doorways of their longhouses and quickly drew back inside. Children stopped their games and ran to their mothers as he approached the village.

The old man was exhausted and hungry. His stomach was a dry and empty cavern. He dragged his feet to the nearest longhouse and knocked on the wooden wall. Eventually a woman appeared hesitantly from behind the deerskin door.

'I have travelled far and am in great need of food and shelter,' he said, so quietly that the woman had to bend forwards to hear him.

Her face became hardened at his words, and she replied, 'Though my heart wishes to make you welcome, my head knows that we have suffered a harsh winter. I have no food to offer you.'

The old man turned away and continued through the village. He came to the next longhouse and once more knocked on the wooden wall. Another woman drew back her deerskin door and stared at him with suspicious eyes.

'I have travelled far and am in great need of food and shelter,' he said in an even quieter voice.

The woman cupped a hand to her ear in order to hear him. But when she did, her face set. She replied, 'Though my heart wishes to make you welcome, my head knows that we have suffered a harsh winter. I have no food to offer you.'

The old man went on his way, stopping at each longhouse with his simple request, and at each one it was refused by the woman who answered.

Finally he arrived at the last house. Before he could even raise his hand to knock on the wall, the deerskin door was thrown back and a woman rushed out to meet him. Without a word she took him in her arms and helped him to a seat by the fire. 'We don't have much,' she said, 'but you have greater need than I of the little that's left.' And she poured her last helping of soup into a bowl and placed her last crust of bread on a plate and gave them to the old man.

He ate slowly and gratefully. Then the woman led him to her bed, where he immediately lay down and fell asleep. He stayed there a whole week, waking for a short time each day to eat the food she was able to find for him.

At the end of the week he rose from the bed and went to sit at her table. But much to the woman's surprise, the old man didn't look at all well. She had expected him to be healed, but instead he was very ill. Concern rose in her face as she led him back to bed. What was wrong with him? What could she do? She had no extra food and she knew no cures. In despair she wrung her hands and said to him, 'What can I do? How can I save you?'

The old man opened his eyes a little and whispered some words to her. He told her of a place in the corner of the meadow where there grew a certain herb. He told her to go and fetch some of the herb, and then gave her instructions on how to prepare it. After this was done, he swallowed the preparation. By morning he was well.

But by evening he had been taken ill once more, this time with another illness. Again the woman wrung her hands, not knowing how to help. The old man beckoned her to him with a limp hand and directed her to a different part of the meadow, a different herb and a different preparation. After this was done, he swallowed the mixture and by morning he was restored to health.

But as this day drew to a close, a third illness took hold and pulled him back down on to the bed. As before, he had the woman mix up a cure, a different one this time, which worked as expected.

For many moons this pattern of events continued until he had outrun every illness that stalked humankind. From then on he lived a simple, healthy life in the woman's longhouse, speaking little and helping with the chores as he was able.

Then one day, as the woman was returning from her garden, she saw a fierce white glow coming from behind her longhouse. The deerskin door dissolved away and there stood a handsome young man dressed in white buckskin. As he walked towards her with strong, rhythmic strides, the glow came with him. Somehow the woman knew that this was the old man, transformed into his true self. He was the peace-maker. With a voice of deep crystal rivers and dark amber syrup be spoke to her, 'I came to Earth to test the people – to see if they remembered the teachings about hospitality. Only you remembered what should have been done, so in return I bestow on you a wonderful gift that will bring others to you in their greatest need and earn you the respect of many.'

And then he began to rise up into the sky, leaving the woman wondering what the gift might be.

Let's create

Native American Indian folklore carries history, wisdom and culture – including natural methods of healing. 'The Hidden Gift' and several other stories in this book are inspired by legends of the Iroquois tribe. The gift received by the kind woman is the ability to heal. We'll use this starting place to create fantasy medicines for some interesting childhood illnesses.

Cover basic safety around medicines before starting. Make it totally clear to all your learners that this is a make-believe activity.

Be sensitive to children in the class who have or have had illnesses.

Learners will create

A fantasy medicine box that holds cures for uncommon childhood illnesses

Learners will develop

A belief that creativity can be a natural response to pain, suffering and boredom

A belief that creativity can change and improve things

An ability to make, think or do things that haven't been made, thought or done before

You will need

Copies of the Medicine Bottles sheet and the Curious Childhood Illnesses list (see pp. 125 and 126)

Main activity

- Share the story, allow learners to respond freely, then ask:
  - What gift does the woman receive?
  - Why does the old man transform?
  - What if all illness could be cured?
- Share with your learners the Curious Childhood Illnesses list (p. 126)
- Suggest the name for a medicine that could cure 1 of the illnesses – e.g. Sunday fever could be soothed by Frydai cream, and Time flu by clock pills
- Make sure that each cure is related to the illness
- Challenge learners to create medicines to cure the illnesses, writing their names on the medicine bottles

Plenary

- Learners share their medicine bottles with each other, guessing which medicine cures which illness
- Ask learners if they:
  - were able to think up appropriate names for medicines easily
  - think that creativity can solve problems and make life better
  - believe that doctors are creative
- Record their comments publicly where they can be referred to easily

Support, extension and application

For younger or emerging creators:

- List medicines that learners have seen or used; review safety around medicines
- Limit the fantasy illnesses to the simple and humorous ones
- Create medicines and ask learners to match them to illness

For older or more experienced creators:

- Devise a treatment schedule for each illness
- Create combinations of medicines – pills, powders, potions, creams, etc.
- Describe new illnesses – with names such as ear gibbets, cringle tubes, snave arms, back spangs, gloobles, quarter breath

Applications

Now and again it's wise to have a bit of fun rather than force connections to the National Curriculum

The Tale of Willy Woodknock

Willy Woodknock was hiking over the mountain to see his sweetheart Caragh Dew. She lived with her mother in the next village. It was the first day of May and the air was as clear as the chime of a new church bell. Willy hummed a merry tune because he expected that Caragh would offer to kiss him today.

At the top of the mountain he looked back and saw his own village down in the valley. The cottages were like sugar cubes scattered on a green plate. Looking the other way, he could see Caragh's village in the next valley. It wasn't yet mid-day and the path was easy from now on, so he decided to rest a while and think a little more about his beloved. There was plenty of time, so Willy took off his rucksack, fished inside it for a snack of bread and cheese and a flask of wine, then lay down on the warm grassy slope. The hot sun and a full stomach soon sent Willy into a comfortable sleep.

When he awoke, many hours later, the sun was just about to sink below the horizon and the air had turned icy. And there was now someone with him on the lonely mountainside. A peculiar shape in silhouette squatted on a rock several metres away. It seemed to be looking towards him, but he wasn't sure. Willy felt uneasy, so he jumped up, quickly gathered his things and was about to head off when the shadow spoke:

Caragh waits upon the cottage step,

Tapping foot and frowning.

Wonders where her true love's gone,

Wishes he was adrowning.

Willy's heart missed a beat. What was this creature? How did it know so much about him? Had he lost Caragh's favour? Was she that angry with him for being a few hours late? The creature continued:

If through the mountain door we go

(A trick to turn back time)

Then Caragh will forget your sin,

And your love will surely shine!

Willy was anxious. He didn't want to lose Caragh's love, but could he trust this odd creature to help him? It hopped down from the rock and hurried off. What should Willy do? He had to decide quickly because the creature was disappearing into the gloom. Willy followed it to a small wooden door set in the hillside. He was nearer to the creature now, but its features were no sharper. He could make out only a vague shape that was the colour of nightfall.

As the sun finally set and the stars began to shine, it opened the door and Willy followed it inside to a low circular tunnel lined with wood. The creature ran on ahead and disappeared. Willy went after it, his shoes going 'knock, knock, knock, knock' on the tunnel floor. After a while the way divided in two, but the creature was nowhere to be seen. One route headed upwards and the other down. Willy chose to go down, thinking of Caragh's village in the valley below. His heart beat furiously and his breaths became short and full of panic. 'Knock, knock, knock, knock' went his shoes as the route divided again. Down or up? Down, of course. 'Knock, knock, knock, knock.'

Up or down? Down, of course. On and on and on he ran, and for all I know he's running to this day, desperately trying to find the door so he can escape and find his love, Caragh.

So, if you're ever out for a walk in the mountains on the first day of May, lay down and press your ear to the grass. You just might hear an odd noise: 'Knock, knock, knock, knock', the sound of Willy's shoes. Maybe it's getting louder – Willy's getting closer to where you are. Or maybe as you listen it becomes faint and dies away to silence. But while you listen, whatever you do, don't fall asleep on the warm grass.

Let's create

We'll use this story as raw material for some creative wordplay

Learners will create

A wordplay that compares and arranges various sets of words from the story in creative ways

Learners will develop

An ability to use both analytic and holistic thinking

An ability to make, think or do things that haven't been made, thought or done before

A belief that creative potential is inside everyone and may be found everywhere

You will need

Paper, pens, copies of the story (a version may be downloaded from www.thinkingclassroom.co.uk)

Main activity

- Share the story, allow learners to respond freely, then ask:

  - What words suggest that Willy's in trouble?

  - Why does Willy take a nap?

  - What if Willy eventually escaped from his underground prison?

- Learners take a copy of the story and randomly highlight 5 common nouns from different parts of the story (e.g. mountain, shadow, door, walk, ear)

- Carry out 1 or more of the following wordplays:

  - Which of the 5 words is the least expensive, least useful, least durable, least silly, least human – and other leasts?

  - Order the words from 1 to 5 by the criteria above

  - Rank the words by the criteria above (when ranking, 2 or more words may have the same importance)

  - Which word is the odd 1 out?

  - Create 2 pairs of words, each having something in common

  - Create a pair and a trio of words, each having something in common

  - Choose 2 words and say how 1 could improve the other – e.g. How could an ear improve a door?

  - Repeat the other way round – e.g. How could a door improve an ear?

  - Using the version of the story, play around with the Find/Replace editing features to make global changes – e.g. change all 'Willy's to your own name

- Choose 5 different words and repeat

Plenary

- Share wordplay results
- Ask learners if they can invent any other wordplay activities
- Ask learners if they:

  - created new ideas using wordplay

  - found ideas in unexpected places (i.e. in the 5 simple words)

- Record their comments publicly where they can be referred to easily

Support, extension and application

For younger or emerging creators:

- Choose 3 familiar related words (e.g. bread, cheese, wine)

- Look for 1 common feature between 2 words

- Focus on 1 paragraph of the story

For older or more experienced creators:

- Work with 10 words

- Use complex comparisons – e.g. least loving, least hopeless

- Create new wordplays and apply them to abstract nouns/adverbs/verb/adjectives instead of common nouns

Applications

All subjects require familiarity with core keywords. Select these keywords and apply wordplay techniques to them.

Avani

A long time ago and a very long way away there was a planet called Avani. It orbited a bright yellow sun whose rays kept the Avanians happy and caused their crops to grow very tall indeed. All was well on Avani: music was made, stories were told, families shared food around tables, laughter was everywhere, and each person was content with a simple and peaceful life. But then the machines came and the trouble began.

First to arrive were the Steamers, dropping through the clouds like smoking black eggs. They thudded into the ground and cracked open with a rush of oily vapour. Inside each egg the Avanians found a strange contraption made from shining steel and polished wood. Wheels spun, boilers puffed, gears shifted and the Steamers rattled and clattered out into Avani.

At first the Avanians were wary of these noisy visitors, but after a time they grew to like them. Each Steamer was in some way helpful in daily life. Some could be ridden, and the time to travel between villages was halved; some of them could plough fields and sow seeds, which meant that twice as much land was planted with food crops; some could drill down into Avani's soft crust, where glittering stones and sparkling metals were discovered. These were brought to the surface to much ooing and aahing from the awestruck Avanians.

The Avanians couldn't believe what they had been missing. Now they could speed along at 10 miles per hour. So what if a Steamer crashed now and again and someone died? Now they had twice as much food on their plates. So what if a few of them put on a bit of weight and became ill? Now they had valuable jewels and metals. So what if a few people stole each other's treasures once in a while? Life was different. It was faster and more exciting. OK, so it was a little noisier with a little less laughter too, but on the whole the Avanians were better off, weren't they?

When the Steamers were no longer a novelty, the Silicas appeared. They sped down through the clouds in sleek white spaceships. When the Avanians plucked up the courage to look inside, they gasped in amazement. Each Silica was covered with flickering coloured lights and flashing screens. Each one had legs and arms with many joints and wonderful tools attached to the ends.

The Silicas glided out on to Avani and began their work. Some floated through the air so the Avanians could travel right round their planet and look down on its beauty; some created new and tasty foods from waste. The Avanians quickly took a liking to this. Some of the Silicas built cities full of towering buildings with mirrored outsides and glamorous insides. The Avanians swiftly abandoned their villages and went to live in these new places.

The Avanians couldn't believe what they had been missing. The Steamers were forgotten and lay rusting in the abandoned villages. Now the Avanians could fly. So what if the clouds were burned now and then? Now they had exotic foods. So what if a few of them carried terrible diseases? Now they had cities. So what if a few people went mad with anger at living so close to other Avanians? Life was different. It was much faster and far more exciting. OK, so it was a lot noisier with much less laughter, but on the whole the Avanians were better off, weren't they?

And finally the Noos arrived. They just appeared one day, clumps of grey matter, boiling and squirming around on themselves, like brains rearranging their parts.

The Avanians picked up the Noos and, when they did, each Noo scuttled up a sleeve or a trouser leg and settled on the back of an Avanian. The Noos began to whisper into the Avanians' ears. With the Noos' help, each Avanian could now think at the speed of light and listen in to the ideas of other Avanians. Any problem was solved in a heartbeat. The Noos could also reshape matter. If an Avanian wanted to become smaller or taller or wider or take on the form of a tree, all it took was a thought and the Noos twisted their body into its new shape.

Life was different. It was lived at the speed of light and was far too exciting. OK, so it was silent and there were no laughter or emotions, but on the whole the Avanians were better off, weren't they?

The Avanians soon came to believe that they were the most important race in the universe. All they needed to do now was prove it. The Noos turned them into spacecraft and they set off into the skies. I wonder if they'll ever arrive here. Or maybe they already have …

Let's create

Of course, Avani bears more than a passing resemblance to Earth, and hopefully your children will notice this. The story provides a prompt for discussing human development, evolution, history, technological progress, global warming, and so on, but we'll use it here more directly to demonstrate a useful random creative process.

Learners will create

A new alien by randomly combining elements of the Steamers, Silicas and Noos using a 6 x 6 grid and two dice

Learners will develop

An attitude of positivity towards surprising and unexpected events

A belief that creativity can change things and improve things

An ability to make, think or do things that haven't been made, thought or done before

You will need

Copies of the Alien Creator Grid (see p. 127), dice, materials with which to make new aliens – e.g. for 2D representations: painting/drawing, for 3D modelling: sculpture/junk modelling

Main activity

- Share the story, allow learners to respond freely, then ask:
    - What effect did the alien visitors have on the Avanians?
    - Why did the Avanians need to prove their superiority?
    - What if they found they visited the Silicas' home planet?
- Review the features of the three types of Alien visitor – Steamer, Silica and Noo
- Demonstrate the Alien Creator Grid:
    - throw 2 dice 6 times to select randomly 6 features taken from all 3 races combined
    - discuss if anything further needs to be added to make the new alien realistic
    - allow up to 2 extras or 1 rethrow (to replace any 1–2 of the 6 features) if the design is tricky to make
- Ask learners to generate their own new aliens and then make them (you will have decided earlier whether they will draw, paint, sculpt, model, etc. their creations)
- Set to work making the aliens

Plenary

- Ask learners to display their work next to the Alien Creator Grid used for its design

- Allow learners to look at each other's creations and evaluate whether or not they have the features on the grid

- Ask learners if they:

  - found it easy to accept the features suggested by the roll of the dice

  - have made something original

  - have made an alien that is better than either a Steamer, Silica or Noo

- Record their comments publicly where they can be referred to easily

Support, extension and application

For younger or emerging creators:

- Simplify the grid

- Provide a simple starting point and ask learners to add 2 or 3 interesting features

- Create new animals from the parts of 3 well-known ones

For older or more experienced creators:

- Add more challenging features to the grid, such as, 'can smell things 1000 miles away', 'always looks sad'

- Make additional requirements – e.g. 10 features to be included – with no option to add further features or change any of the 10

- Evaluate new aliens against agreed criteria such as 'danger to Avanians', 'usefulness', 'good or evil'

Applications

A 6 x 6 grid and 2 dice is a wonderful example of structured creativity and may be used wherever ideas (within defined limits) are needed quickly. Examples are the following grids:

Mathematics
- numbers to generate new problems

Language and communication
- words to generate new story ideas

Science and technology
- features to generate new products

Art and design
- colours and shapes to generate new pieces of art

Health and well-being
- foods to generate new diets

Human, social and environmental
- buildings to generate new settlements

The Wizard of Burnham Market

The best wizards have the best disguises. They don't want any old fool pestering them for magic spells, so they take great care to look nothing like wizards. The wizard of Burnham Market (Ben to his friends, Kered to the rest of the world – all part of the disguise) was especially good at looking unwizardlike, and he was an especially powerful wizard.

Ben was the wizard to whom all the other wizards turned for advice – whether this was about magic or about their business ventures or about their personal affairs. Ben was also the wizard with the most apprentices and the one who had created the world-famous three rules of magic. If you know anything about real magic, you'll have heard of these rules, but here they are anyway – remember, it was Ben who invented them:

1. Never tell anyone that you are a wizard.

2. Any magic you attempt must always be for the benefit of other people.

3. Never accept payment for magic (it stops the spell working).

Ben also invented the three guidelines for making magic work:

When you operate your magic:

1. Don't try to make it work – the more you try, the less powerful it is.

2. Always make a clear image of it in your mind.

3. Always check with a more experienced wizard first.

You'd think magic was quite simple – only three rules and only three guidelines – but it isn't. Non-wizards should steer well clear of it!

One day a rich and evil merchant recognised Ben for what he truly was. He saw through the disguise and decided he could use Ben's knowledge to make even more money. So that night he broke into Ben's home and stole his notebook.

Back in the study of his huge mansion, he flicked through the pages of the stolen book and chuckled. There must be a hundred fortunes here, he thought. He had discovered Ben's ideas for new magic – magic that no one else knew. The idea that really caught his eye involved thinking about the Earth in a slightly different way and then using the difference to power a vehicle. This vehicle could transport you to wherever you wanted to go – in less time than it took to unpack a wand.

Immediately, the rich and evil merchant began thinking about the world in this slightly different way, following the directions and diagrams in Ben's notebook. After a few minutes he had accumulated more than enough difference to enchant a small bicycle – which he did right away.

With simply the power of thought, the bicycle took him to a small planet called Syrius. And with another thought he came right back again. He thought about last week and the bicycle flicked him back seven days in time. He conjured an image of seven days into the future and he was back in the present again.

Then he began to make money: travelling quietly into the secret meetings of other merchants, pedalling a little forwards in time to find out what decisions people made, and moving a little backwards in time to undo his mistakes and slightly alter his business decisions.

After a month of this, he had become the richest man on the planet. People knew he had money, but this extra wealth was very mysterious.

Of course, Ben had realised that his notebook had gone and within minutes he had used his most powerful magic to identify the thief. But, quite unexpectedly, he had done nothing to retrieve it. In the month when it had been in the hands of the greedy merchant, Ben had been sitting at home drinking Vanilla Chai (a wizard's drink) and chuckling quietly to himself. I wonder why that was?

Let's create

Ben, the wizard of Burnham Market, is waiting for the thief to make a simple mistake. Then he will quietly walk in and retrieve his notebook. The merchant is so greedy that he is about to make too much money – more money than there is in the world. This of course will come to the attention of the authorities, who will send him to a very dark prison.

The magic done in this story is impossible (at the moment), but imagining the impossible is an important and useful creative activity. Thinking up impossible things is straightforward. All we need to do is start with something possible and extend one or more feature again and again. For example: I can cycle to the shops (possible) – I can cycle to Manchester (possible) – I can cycle to Afghanistan (possible but not advisable) – I can cycle to the moon (impossible) – I can cycle to another universe (impossible). Here the element of distance has been extended until impossibility rules.

Learners will create

An impossibility that takes existing ideas to interesting new realms

Learners will develop

An ability to see familiar things in new and different ways

An attitude of openness to new ideas and experiences when they appear

You will need

Nothing

Main activity

- Share the story, allow learners to respond freely, then ask:
  - What rules does magic have?
  - Why does Ben not chase the merchant?
  - What if we could all do impossible things?
- Learners together generate a list of possible actions or true statements – e.g. I can eat 1 sandwich in 5 minutes / Cheese is made from cow's milk
- Choose an action or statement from the list and select 1 of its features
- Extend this feature a little to see if the statement is still true
- Keep extending until it is impossible, very impossible and then totally ludicrous

Plenary

- Compare impossible statements to find the most impossible
- Ask learners if they:
  - were happy to create impossible ideas
  - can use this way of thinking to generate new ideas in different subjects
- Record their comments publicly where they can be referred to easily

Support, extension and application

For younger or emerging creators:

- Find magic and impossible events in familiar stories
- Remove the need to increase the impossibility gradually
- Sort ideas into possible and impossible

For older or more experienced creators:

- Create a 11-point scale (–5 to +5) from possibility to impossibility for a chosen idea
- Research ideas that were once impossible but no longer are – e.g. remote (wireless) communication
- Survey the use of magic in literature

Applications

Impossible statements in various subjects provide useful thinking challenges to help clarify the possible. For example, learners can try to prove that the following are impossible:

Mathematics

- $2 + 2 = 5$

Language and communication

- There are 120,000 languages spoken in the world

Science and technology

- People can travel faster than light

Art and design

- Furniture can hover if asked to

Health and well-being

- No one is overweight

Human, social and environmental

- Historical characters often visit the present

The Princess who could see Everything

The King and Queen of Bermingham had waited such a very long time for their first child that they began to wonder if one would ever come along. However, one clear winter's day Princess Millie was born, and at last the King and Queen were able to sigh with relief. The whole kingdom rejoiced and threw a party that lasted until the end of the next summer.

Millie grew up into a bright-eyed, rosy-cheeked little girl with a good warm heart and a sensible head. She was a blessing to her parents and a joy to her nurses. As the years sped by, beauty blossomed in her face and many skills passed into her fingers. She learned quickly and by the age of 18 it seemed that there was nothing she couldn't do. It was a little while later that Millie announced she had decided to marry. Right away a queue of eager young men appeared at the palace gates, but Millie was not a prize that was easily won.

Of all her wonderful qualities perhaps the most curious was her uncanny ability to see everything. Millie had been able to do this since she was a toddler (Hide and Seek had never been much fun with her), and she thought it would be wise to use it now to choose her husband. 'Marrying me is simple,' she laughed at the men. 'All you must do is hide so that I cannot find you!'

The suitors were really enthusiastic and tried their very best to put themselves out of Millie's sight. They rushed off to hide in ditches and behind hedges, in cellars and attics and priest holes, in caves, over mountains, up trees and locked in towers. But Princess Millie had the eyes of a goddess. She could see everything! She could see all those unfortunate men just by looking in their general direction.

The next batch of potential husbands gave the task a bit more thought. They'd heard about the first lot. They hid in ships or behind animals or under wigs or behind false beards or at the back of very thick buildings. But Princess Millie found all of them just as easily as before.

More and more men tried to pass Millie's test. They travelled farther away and got into deeper and darker places. But it was no good. She found them all.

Eventually only three poor brothers remained. Millie wasn't hopeful as she looked at their patched clothes and innocent, eager faces. But she smiled kindly and told the eldest brother to go and hide from her. Off he went, and after an hour she began to look for him.

He wasn't in a ditch or behind a hedge. He wasn't down a cellar or up in an attic. Nor was he in a priest hole, in a cave, up a mountain, behind a tree or locked in a tower. She was impressed. No one had stayed hidden this long before. But just then she cast her gaze into the sky and there he was, hiding behind the sun.

The middle brother set off, and after an hour Millie began to look again. He wasn't on a ship or behind an animal or under a wig or behind a false beard. And he certainly wasn't at the back of any very thick building. Millie was impressed. He'd stayed hidden longer than his older brother. But just then she looked down and there he was, hiding at the very centre of the Earth.

The youngest brother took his turn. All Millie's plans rested on him. She rather hoped he'd succeed because he was by far the most attractive man she'd seen since she decided to get married. He set off, and after an hour she began to look for him. She looked in all the obvious places. She looked behind the sun and down at the centre of the Earth. She peered into deserts and behind stars. She stared into deep seas and checked the dark side of the moon, but by bedtime she still had not found him. She was both concerned and excited. She hoped he would remain hidden so she could marry him, but if he never returned she wouldn't be able to.

Millie wandered through the garden and back towards the palace. She stopped to pick a rose and put it into her hair. In her rooms her ladies-in-waiting greeted her and began to prepare her for bed. Millie was lost in thought. Where could the youngest brother have gone? Just before she got into bed, she reached up to her hair to remove the rose. She jumped with fright as she felt a warm hand there. The youngest brother stepped out of the rose and climbed down to the floor.

'I chose to hide in the garden, in the rose I knew you'd pick,' he said. They embraced. Millie was more than happy to marry such a clever man. But she knew he'd never be able to hide from her again!

Let's create

This story is based on a classic Hungarian fairy tale. It provides a great opportunity for developing the use of senses in creativity. What would it be like to see flavours or hear textures? Some people live with this type of gift (or affliction). It's called *synesthesia* and is probably a throwback to our first months, when our brains had yet to separate out the different senses.

The wider and deeper your experience, the more source material there is at hand to be creative. It's important therefore to teach young learners to make the most of their senses. Thinking about one sense in terms of another is a rich and engaging way to do this.

Learners will create

A mash-up poem about the senses.

Learners will develop

An ability to make, think or do things that haven't been made, thought or done before

An ability to see familiar things in new and different ways

You will need

Copies of the Mash-up Grid (p. 128)

Main activity

- Share the story, allow learners to respond freely, then ask:
  - Why did Princess Millie choose her husband in the way she did?
  - What hiding places did the suitors try?
  - What if Millie could hear, taste or smell everything?

- Take learners outside and spend time looking, listening, smelling, touching and tasting
- Enrich this activity by challenging them to:
  - sense a target number of things
  - sense as many things as they can in a limited space
  - look intently at an item and describe it in great detail
- Distribute the mash-up grid and explain how it works (example below):
  - draw or write in each box on the left-most column
  - choose 5 empty boxes and in each describe how the image, sound, etc. might appear through a different sense
  - links can be obvious or obscure
- Some of the 20 combinations will work more easily than others; try out more than 5 and select the best
- Create a poem using the suggested structure and ideas from the mash-up grid

Plenary

- Share poems with each other and identify particularly creative lines
- Create group poems – each member of the group contributes their 'best' line
- Ask learners if they:
  - have made or thought things that they've not before
  - have been able to see objects in a different way
- Record their comments publicly where they can be referred to easily

Support, extension and application

For younger or emerging creators:

- Focus the grid/poem on 1 sense
- Suggest objects that have strong associations with more than 1 sense
- Associate a series of colours with tastes or a series of textures with sounds

For older or more experienced creators:

- Create poems about 1 object only, interpreted through 5 senses
- Express abstract concepts through the senses
- Create interesting new senses with which to observe objects – e.g. rinkling (sensing age)

Applications

A mash-up grid provides a process for combining related ideas and therefore creating new ones. The resulting mash-up poem lays down these new ideas in a repeating structure. By altering the column and row prompts the grid can be used in all areas of study:

Mathematics

- Rows: 3D shapes Columns: public buildings

Language and communication

- Rows: methods of communication Columns: purposes of communication

Science and technology

- Rows: materials Columns: day-to-day domestic products

Art and design

- Rows: places to make marks Columns: mark makers

Health and well-being

- Rows: food groups Columns: methods of serving food

Human, social and environmental

- Rows: types of transport Columns: purposes of journeys

	See	Hear	Taste	Touch	Smell
Image: A tree bending in the wind					Rubber tyres
Sound: An old clock ticking			Walnuts and coffee		
Flavour: Apple juice and toast		Clarinets and sandpaper			
Texture: Rough and ridged		tapping			
Aroma: Pine trees				Spikes	

The Sparrow who swallowed a Sunset

Winter was biting hard, like the teeth of a ferocious polar bear clamped on to its latest meal. The land was bare and so terribly cold that humans stayed inside their stone houses all day long, huddled around flickering stoves, waiting for spring to arrive. Rivers froze right the way down to their beds and the earth turned into an icy prison that trapped rabbits, worms and seeds behind its frosty iron bars.

Nybor the sparrow was dreadfully anxious. She was very cold and very hungry. This was all because she was a small and quiet bird who never made a fuss. There was nothing very special about Nybor, nothing to make her noticeable. As far as the other birds were concerned she didn't even exist. So when the humans threw scraps of food out of their windows she was always at the back of the queue. The other birds scrabbled and squabbled for it, but by the time she'd edged her way forwards, everything had been gobbled up.

And at night, when it turned even colder, the birds squeezed together in rows upon the rafters of a nearby barn, but they never made any space for her. She was left shivering and hungry outside on the roof.

One day Nybor looked up into the sky and stared towards the bright watery sun. That must be a warmer place than here, she thought, so she decided to fly away. She summoned her strength, took a deep breath, fluttered her wings and rose into the air. She flew and flew, never taking her eyes off the yellow circle high up in the sky. She was still awfully cold, but the promise of warmth drew her forwards.

As she made her way higher and the day wore on, she noticed that the sun had sunk a little lower in the sky and its bright yellow rays had begun to deepen. She was concerned that the heat she so desperately needed might be fading away, so she beat her wings faster. She hurried on, but seemed to get no nearer to her goal.

Soon the rich yellow light turned to bright orange. Her wing beats began to slow and tiredness crept into his body. She slowed down and lost height until a gust of freezing cold air suddenly snapped her back to life. She was frantic and fluttered furiously. She set her sights once more on the falling sun, but soon Nybor again began to drop lower and lower and her wings lost their rhythm.

She needed the warmth of the sun so badly that she reached deep inside her body and summoned the last of her power. And even as her little wings flapped desperately, the orange glow turned to pink, then red, and the sun dropped on to the horizon. Faster, faster, she thought as the red glow sank farther. It was fading away, just like her. She was so tired she was falling asleep on the wing. Her little heart was beating far too fast.

At last, with a frenzied burst of energy and a whirr of wings, she launched himself into the deep red sunset with her beak wide open, chirping for all she was worth. With this final, tragic act her wings stopped beating and she fell out of the air, dead, like an insignificant brown pebble.

In the morning the sun came up on to a snowy landscape in which there lay a tiny brown speck. Nybor was frozen solid, with her wings tight against her body, but her beak was open as if she were still calling to the sunset.

As the sun's rays fell on to her chest, something changed. Where once she was brown, her chest and throat now glowed a wonderful rich red. And as the sun came higher and higher, Nybor began to soften and her tiny heart began to beat again. The light worked its way through her tiny body and brought her back to life. But no longer was she an insignificant brown sparrow. She had been transformed into a bird with a wonderful red breast. She had swallowed a sunset and it was alive and glowing within her.

Robyn turned away from the sun, proudly lifted her wings, and shot off up into the winter sky.

Let's create

'The Sparrow who swallowed a Sunset' tells a story of striving, death and rebirth. After a life-threatening effort the sparrow dies in achieving her goal but later is transformed into a robin. These are very grown-up themes, so we'll retell the story using a series of images.

Learners will create

A clip stream that retells the story with a series of simple images linked to major themes

Learners will develop

An ability to make, think or do things that haven't been made, thought or done before

An ability to see familiar things in new and different ways

You will need

Access to computers with an extensive clip-art library; copies of the story (downloadable as a Word document from www.thinkingclassroom.co.uk)

Main activity

- Share the story, allow learners to respond freely, then ask:
  - What happened to the sparrow?
  - Why was the sparrow bullied?
  - What if the sparrow didn't come back to life?
- Ensure that learners know how to import and arrange several clip-art images together in (e.g.) a Word document
- Open a copy of the story text and highlight key sentences
- Delete sentences that are not highlighted
- Import a clip-art image to represent (directly or metaphorically) each remaining sentence
- Remove all words and save the series of images

Plenary

- email images to each other and see how well they retell the story

Ask learners if they:
  - made an accurate retelling of the story
  - understand the story better
- Record their comments publicly where they can be referred to easily

Support, extension and application

For younger or emerging creators:

- Provide a set of clip-art images in a file and ask learners to order them to retell the story
- Provide choices of images to use
- Retell a familiar story with images

For older or more experienced creators:

- Retell the story in an exact number of images – 3, 5, 15
- All images must be metaphorical or indirect (e.g. no images of sparrows – use a tiny scared mouse to suggest the sparrow, use a shadow to represent the bullies)
- Recreate a story from a given clip stream

Applications

A series of images may be used to represent processes in different subject areas:

Mathematics

- Represent a multi-part problem

Language and communication

- Represent a well-known story

Science and technology

- Represent the life of a machine – manufacture to decay/recycle

Art and design

- Represent the thoughts of an artist

Health and well-being

- Represent a life

Human, social and environmental

- Represent a period of history

The Paradigm Maverick

There are three things that you need to know about Jamelia Pine. The first is this: that a maverick is a person who thinks in a different way from other people and who often acts in a different way too. There's a very good chance that you're a maverick because you're reading this story rather than tidying your room or weeding the garden.

The second is this: that a paradigm is a way of seeing the world, a pattern of things, a set of expectations about how events will turn out. Scientists (especially physicists) like to keep the word to themselves, but everyone (especially mavericks) is free to use it. In one paradigm everything is possible and you believe that you can achieve anything. In another one everything has limits and you'd better not get ideas above your station. A paradigm like this is a favourite of people who like to inspect other people doing a job rather than doing the job themselves. There are, of course, many other paradigms.

The third and final thing you need to know is this: that Jamelia Pine was the world's greatest paradigm maverick.

So here's the tale of Jamelia Pine.

Jamelia was the only child of two very busy people whose busyness meant that they had no time to pay her any attention. Her father was a well-known brain scientist – you know, the one who discovered which parts of the brain make a person moody, sullen and sulky. Her mother was an author of books about herself, which she wrote continuously in the attic of their large city house. So, apart from the attic, Jamelia had the house pretty much to herself all day and every day. And this gave her plenty of time to think and plenty of time to turn into the sort of person her parents would have been horrified to have in the house – had they ever taken the time to find out what she was like. For Jamelia was a very moody, very sullen and very sulky 10-year-old.

In her lonely hours spent wandering along the many corridors and rooms, her mind learned a rather unusual trick. It learned to detach itself from Jamelia's brain and shift sideways a metre or so. This meant that the dumb grey wrinkly glob of jelly in her skull (brain) travelled a different path from the ghostly network of thoughts that did all the hard work (mind). Jamelia's mind knew that it had left her body, but her brain was blissfully ignorant of the fact.

At first her mind could travel only a short distance, but with patience and practice she eventually managed to send it outside into the street. This was all rather exciting (even for a moody, sullen and sulky teenager) because wherever Jamelia's mind went, there was her awareness. When she was still in the house, she could see and hear and feel as if she was somewhere completely different.

With patience and lots more practice she was able to project her mind into nearby buildings. She came to find out all sorts of things that were nothing to do with her. In the house next door she watched and listened as a small boy crept into his baby sister's room and poked her through the bars of her cot until she cried. The boy sneaked off into his own room before his parents came to soothe her.

Farther down the street she often went to observe a man and woman who were clearly full of bitterness and anger. They didn't have a kind word to say to each other. They nitpicked all day long, criticising each other and bickering.

If she sent her mind towards another person, it was absorbed like water into a dry sponge. Straight away she was able to see the world from the point of view of someone else. This was most interesting – to discover the judgements and prejudices of other people. She could have some fun if she ever met these people for real. She'd know how they thought. Jamelia enjoyed exploring these different paradigms and found that she was free to come and go inside other people's heads.

Imagine her surprise one day when her mind returned home to her head to discover that someone else had taken up residence there. Someone who would not ever let her in again.

Let's create

This story is a twin to 'The House of Loyalty' (p. 88); it explores exactly the same creative idea – that of taking on different points of view, different perspectives. Jamelia invades other people's heads and can see the world as they do. This should be a wonderful gift, but before she can really use it she finds that someone or something else has taken over her own head.

In this activity we'll make simple clay figures (*golems*), each of which has a single, specific world view, and then see what they each think about important topics.

Learners will create

A PoV (point of view) golem – a little clay person with a specific point of view

Learners will develop

An ability to see familiar things in new and different ways

An attitude of openness to new ideas and experiences when they appear

An ability to make, think or do things that haven't been made, thought or done before

You will need

Clay, modelling clay or similar material

Main activity

- Share the story, allow learners to respond freely, then ask:
  - What had entered Jamelia's head?
  - Why did she get so bored?
  - What if she could never get back into her head?
- Explain that people have different opinions and different ways of seeing the same thing or idea
- Give an example – e.g. some people like sport, others don't; both views are fine
- Come up with a list of ways of seeing the world – e.g. :
  - everything is an opportunity
  - everything is a threat
  - everything is funny
  - everything is dangerous
- Ask learners to make a small clay person: a golem (8–10 cm high) with features to represent 1 of these ways of seeing – e.g. everything-is-funny golem will have a big smiling face and funny features (huge hands?)

Plenary

- When the golems are ready, bring them together and ask them what they think about several important issues

- Learners speak for them, like puppeteers

- Choose relevant issues such as:

  - taking a test

  - eating a large meal

  - fighting in the playground

- Ask learners if:

  - they have become better at appreciating different points of view

- Record their comments publicly where they can be referred to easily

Support, extension and application

For younger or emerging creators:

- Create simple golems – the world is good/bad/happy, etc.

- Ask the golems to talk about themselves before they comment on anything else

- Make golem twins to help each other think

For older or more experienced creators:

- Create golems with complex and changeable personalities

- Make golems debate world issues

- Create visiting golems from different parts of the world

Applications

A core set of golems can be used to think about big issues in different subjects. A good basic set could be:

- It can be done

- It's impossible

- I have an idea

- Who can help us?

The House of Loyalty

The city of the Flat Kings was once a beautiful and wealthy place. Prosperous citizens strode through its mosaic-tiled streets, lined with shops and stalls where white-robed merchants called out and offered jewels, spices and ingenious mechanical toys. A river wide, deep and blue curled slowly between buildings adorned with fine carvings and brightened by colourful murals. Seven sturdy bridges reached their way over the river and arched over the fine ships that passed under them, heading for the sea. The city grew tall and straight as its people grew happier and richer. However, one day an army bearing guns and bombs and utter loyalty to its commander walked unchallenged into the city and changed everything.

The commander chose the city's finest house for himself and moved in. The woman who had been living there complained bitterly. He told her that as he was now the most important person in the city, he could have whatsoever he chose and he had chosen this house. He added that he had named it the House of Loyalty and that loyalty was exactly what he demanded from her right now. She argued with him from the pavement, so he invited her back into the house, then down into the cellar, and promptly made her disappear.

The commander and his army settled into the city like an anvil sinking into a pillow. The mosaic-tiled streets became grey and quiet, the river turned brown, and no more ships dipped their masts under the iron spans of the bridges.

The army ruled through fear. Total loyalty was rewarded with extra food and a low position in the army itself. Disloyalty, even a wayward thought or a loose-tongued word, was punished by a visit to the House of Loyalty. The citizens came to realise that there was no homecoming after this kind of visit.

Then a different army appeared and marched into the city. They came seeking gold and jewels. The battle that followed was so intense that all of the buildings of the city tipped over by a few degrees – all except the House of Loyalty, which remained upright, tall and menacing.

The citizens rejoiced and sang songs to their liberators – for about an hour, which was the time it took them to realise that this army was worse than the first. The new commander moved into the House of Loyalty and his soldiers set to work running the city like those before them, except that this time loyalty was to the new commander, not the old.

Some brave souls formed their own army in secret. But it was small and badly organised and the real army crushed it in seconds. The rebels quickly found themselves in the cellar of the House of Loyalty and, soon after, were to be found no more. The new army persuaded some of the citizens that their commander was kind and good and only wanted the best for the city, but the evidence did not bear this out. The city became greyer and darker and was harder to live in, especially since all the buildings had shifted over more in the fighting.

Then a third army arrived. Yet again the commander had heard tales of wonderful riches and wanted them for himself. The battle that followed was even more vicious than before and all of the buildings of the city tipped over by another few degrees. All except the House of Loyalty, which remained upright, tall and menacing.

It got worse. Over the next few months armies took and retook the city of the Flat Kings time and time again. Each time the fighting was worse than before. Each time the buildings bent a little more until eventually they were almost horizontal – all except the House of Loyalty, which remained upright, tall and menacing.

How could the citizens of the city of the Flat Kings rid themselves of these terrible armies? How could they save their beloved city?

Then a little boy lay down on the grass in a park next to the House of Loyalty, and in a flash of inspired thought saw the answer straight away. Everyone was mistaken. Everyone had been looking at things in the wrong way. It wasn't that the city buildings had been tipped over to the ground by months of fighting, leaving the House of Loyalty upright. It was the other way round. All the buildings were just fine. It was the House of Loyalty that had nearly fallen.

Once word got round and the people started looking at things in this way, a fierce new hope bloomed in their hearts. An angry crowd gathered at the House of Loyalty and surged forwards. As they pushed the building to the ground, it seemed to heave a sigh of relief before crumbling into dust. The latest occupying army no longer had a place of power and fear, so they ran away soon after, leaving the city of the Flat Kings once more at peace, ready to regain its lost wealth and damaged pride.

Let's create

This story is a rather indulgent and not-quite-true caricature of the history of Budapest. 'The House of Loyalty' is inspired by the curious and very real House of Terror Museum at Andrássy út 60. This story introduces the idea that looking at things in a slightly different way may have a huge knock-on impact – a theme that is extended in 'The Paradigm Maverick' (p. 84).

In this activity we'll begin to learn the skills of having a slight shift in perspective in order to help us appreciate different points of view and to give creative insights.

Learners will create

A PoV (point of view) sketch that prompts learners to consider things in a different way.

Learners will develop

An ability to see familiar things in new and different ways

An attitude of openness to new ideas and experiences when they appear

You will need

Paper and pencils

Main activity

- Share the story, allow learners to respond freely, then ask:
    - What was each army looking for?
    - Why were the citizens unable to protect their city?
    - What if the House of Loyalty turned inside out?
- Sketch a quick and simple skyline for the city of the Flat Kings, clearly showing the House of Loyalty straight and every other building leaning over the same way by the same amount
- Ask learners to sketch the little boy's view (House of Loyalty tilted, all other buildings upright)
- Pair up and get each pair to choose an area in the place you're in
- One of each pair sits upright and sketches the area
- The other lays down on their side and sketches the same area at an angle

or

- Pair up and choose a non-symmetrical object
- Each person sketches the object from a different position

Plenary

- Pairs of pairs get together and share their sketches
- Ask learners if:
    - it matters where an area or an object was sketched from
    - all views of an area or object are equally valuable
- Record their comments publicly where they can be referred to easily

Support, extension and application

For younger or emerging creators:

- Sketch simple and familiar objects
- Sketch 2 buildings – 1 upright and 1 tilted
- Ask what learners think about a familiar object – e.g. a torch – and note different opinions

For older or more experienced creators:

- Learners adopt an opposing point of view on an important subject (different from their preferred PoV)
- Individually sketch an object from 3 or more different places
- Look at the spaces between objects rather than at the objects themselves

Applications

Empathy and the ability to take on / appreciate different points of view is an essential skill for success in the twenty-first century. Approach it through different subjects. Some simple ideas here:

Mathematics

- Look at several shapes close together and then at the space between them

Language and communication

- Listen to the words in a conversation and then to the pauses between different talkers

Science and technology

- Focus on the noise of machines at home and then on the times when there is relative quiet

Art and design

- Focus on a public statue and then on the buildings/objects nearest to it

Health and well-being

- Focus on a supermarket shelf and then on gaps on the shelf

Human, social and environmental

- Focus on a timeline and then on the parts of it with no important dates

The Maige Bird

By a cold grey rock on top of a tall snowy mountain, higher than anyone has ever climbed, perches the Maige Bird. Still as a pond, hard as stone and the size of a child, he sits alert all day long, letting the icy light fall into his glassy eyes and distant sounds into his funnel ears. Feathers of steel fan out from his tail and glint in the sun while he watches and listens. From this high up, the Maige Bird sees all the world's secrets and hears all the world's whispers. And deep inside each of his metal feathers he collects every last ripple that comes to his ears and every last wrinkle that reaches his eyes. Pluck one feather from his tail and the world is yours: within that feather lies the power to control other people – it will tell you exactly what they have hidden away, exactly what they have tried to keep secret.

Naturally, many people have sought the Maige Bird – rich and poor, evil and good, capable and cynical, curious – but up to now he's kept all his tail feathers safe and sound and firmly attached. For now, that is, but not for much longer …

Mutti is a very rich, very evil and very cynical old man. Over the years his wicked schemes have sucked bags of money from the darkest, dirtiest corners of Earth. He doesn't believe in the Maige Bird — or in any sort of myth or magic, for that matter. But he likes to be 100 per cent certain of things and loves to prove other people wrong – especially if they then have to give him money. So the reason that we now find Mutti seven-eighths of the way up a tall snowy mountain, in search of a grey rock and a mythical bird, is that he wants to show all those magic, floppy-minded folks that there is no such thing as the Maige Bird. He has made a bet with them – half of his wealth says this bird doesn't exist.

Being rich and evil, he has bought or stolen the best equipment ever for a climb such as this and has bullied the most capable guides into leading the way. 'More speed!' he cries into the cold thin air. 'Look, still no stupid magic bird!' he sneers to his panting bag carriers.

And then, fifteen-sixteenths of the way up the tall snowy mountain, Mutti sees something flash in the sunlight ahead. (The Maige Bird has wriggled its tail.) 'A trick of the light, nothing more,' he murmurs quietly, 'a flash in the pan.' But later, thirty-one thirty-seconds from the top, he can't ignore the bird-shaped silhouette standing stone still by a cold grey rock. 'A decoy, nothing more,' he states firmly, 'a statue placed by those magic floppy-minded folks.'

At the top of the tall snowy mountain, Mutti finds he has to do some quick readjustments inside his mind:

1. The Maige Bird does exist.

2. All his guides and carriers have seen it.

3. Half his wealth is at risk.

So Mutti does the only thing that a truly rich and evil old man can do. He commands his guides and carriers to line up at the edge of a big drop just behind the Maige Bird and orders them to jump off. This they do immediately because he is pointing a very large gun at them and they would rather risk the drop.

Then he turns the same very large gun towards the Maige Bird and starts to pull the trigger.

But he stops.

What if it's true? What if those tail feathers really do contain all the secrets and whispers of the world? Mutti changes his plan and slowly approaches the Maige Bird from behind with his non-gun hand outstretched. He gets within a wingspan of the nearest tail feather, and then the bird turns. Mutti goes to the side and is once again behind the bird. He gets closer and lunges. As he pulls a feather free, he shoots the Maige Bird in its chest. Sadly, Mutti is so, so evil that he's having a terrible influence in this story and the bird dies there and then.

Clutching his feather and ignoring the fallen bird, Mutti holds it close up and begins to see names whirling and snaking around on the surface. He holds it close to his ear and starts to hear voices – quiet, furtive, hush-hush voices, making secret plans. He sees the name and hears the voice of another rich and evil man he knows whose money he wants, and he finds out where this man has hidden his gold. He laughs and looks again. Yes! There is a secret that belongs to his brother – his brother has stolen food to feed his family (he is very poor). What fun Mutti can have revealing this knowledge to the police. And oh, what's this? He looks closer still at the wondrous feather ... the name of a guide ... one whom he's just had jump to his death. What secret can a mere mountain climber have ... a secret about the Maige Bird ... a story passed down through his family from great-grandmother, grandmother, mother and finally to this man ... knowledge about the bird ... should anyone kill it ... then ... then ... it will ... then ... it becomes ... oh no ... oh no ... no ...

Let's create

Several meaty themes present themselves in this story: good versus evil, honesty, loyalty and ornithology for a start. We'll combine these into a creative classroom centrepiece that provide ongoing opportunities to wrestle with some of life's big issues.

Learners will create

A maige bird with customised feathers. One or more maige birds are constructed. Each colourful feather includes an interesting thought. More feathers can be added periodically. Success criteria for a maige bird and its feathers are given here, but be guided by rather than restricted by them.

A maige bird:

❶ is inspired by the story

❷ is colourful and attention grabbing

❸ is constructed from junk materials

❹ stands, hangs or perches unaided

❺ will accept new feathers easily

A maige bird feather:

❶ will easily stick into a maige bird and stay there

❷ resembles a real feather

❸ is colourful

❹ has a response to 1 of the following written clearly on it: a big question, a useful secret, wise words, a clever joke, an interesting idea, an interesting thing to do, a great place to go

Learners will develop

An ability to make, think or do things that haven't been made, thought or done before

A belief that creativity can change things and improve things

You will need

A selection of junk materials

Materials for the feathers

Examples of interesting thoughts, e.g:

- A big question – Is success in school the same as success in life?
- A useful secret – You can do the 9-times table with your fingers
- Wise words – A problem shared is a problem halved
- A clever joke – What's brown and sticky? (A stick)
- An interesting idea – What if children only needed 2 hours' sleep each night?
- An interesting thing to do – Try to write with your wrong hand
- A great place to go – Pitt Rivers Museum in Oxford

Main activity 1 (2 sessions and ongoing)

- Share the story, allow learners to respond freely, then ask:
  - Why did Mutti shoot the maige bird?
  - What happened to Mutti at the end of the story?
  - What if there were a bird like the maige bird in our classroom?
- Introduce the project of making a maige bird (or more than 1) and its feathers

- Explain that the class maige bird(s) will get more feathers as we have more interesting and creative thoughts
- Share and adapt the success criteria
- Learners set to work

Main activity 2

- Recap the story and admire the maige bird(s) from previous session
- Check how well it/they meet agreed criteria
- Introduce materials for creating feathers
- Share your interesting thoughts and ask learners to discuss theirs
- Demonstrate making and writing on a feather
- Ask learners to make their own

Plenary

- Stick feathers into the maige bird(s)
- Ask learners if they:
  - have made or thought things that they've not before
  - think that the class maige bird(s) will help others
- Record their comments publicly where they can be referred to easily
- Ask learners when and how they would like to add more feathers

Support, extension and application

For younger or emerging creators:

- Create a maige bird wall display
- Write on the feathers interesting things that learners have seen, heard
- Suggest more familiar animals and ways to attach ideas

For older or more experienced creators:

- Create feathers that are linked creatively
- Make a feather for each of the 7 prompts
- Think up other uses for a maige bird and its feathers

Applications

The class maige bird(s) is meant to be an ongoing repository of creative wisdom. Feathers may be customised to different areas of study:

Mathematics
- Tables, number facts, challenges

Language and communication
- Spelling words, authors and books, made-up words (with definitions)

Science and technology
- Science equipment, wacky chemicals

Art and design
- Colours, ingenious feathers

Health and well-being
- New sports, healthy meals

Human, social and environmental
- Characters from history, ideas for new public buildings

Alfred's Gift

Alfred the snow angel had been banished to Earth. The chief snow angel sent him away because Alfred wasn't like the other angels. They spoke quietly, moved gracefully and made normal snowflakes – ones that followed the rules. Alfred was loud and boisterous and creative. *His* snowflakes were very ingenious but completely forbidden. He'd been warned. He'd been given chances to conform and special responsibilities. He'd even been paired up with Abigail, the chief's favourite. But nothing had worked. Alfred simply couldn't stop being Alfred.

His latest idea had caused a great deal of trouble. Alfred had designed and built a whole day's worth of snowflakes that shouted out fascinating questions in silly voices as they landed on the ground. This upset the people on Earth who had, until Alfred's flakes arrived, been enjoying a beautiful, thought-free and very snowy day. They didn't want to think anything out of the ordinary: just like the snow angels up above, they had their own rules to follow.

How fast does rain go?' shouted the first flake, followed closely by 'How heavy is a smile?' and 'How many leaves are there in the world?' and a thousand thousand more *How* questions. Then came Alfred's *Why* flakes: 'Why are bubbles round?', 'Why do rivers make a noise?', 'Why do mirrors reflect?' and a hundred flurries more. Finally came his finest ones, his *What ifs*: 'What if every thought became a sound?', 'What if there were no night?', 'What if there were no more beetles?' and so on. The people were not used to questions like these. *What*, *When* and *Who* suited them. They complained to the chief snow angel and the chief snow angel had to act. So Alfred found himself wingless, earthbound and hungry.

He wandered through the streets of the town in which he had been dumped, stopping occasionally to peer through shop windows. It was getting dark and he needed to find food and shelter quickly. The other snow angels were being particularly spiteful to Alfred. They were sending down an especially heavy fall of snow, made up of the largest flakes they were allowed to build. Footsteps and cart tracks disappeared in minutes and eventually Alfred could see no farther than a feather's length in front of his face.

Alfred stepped into a doorway to avoid the worst of the snow. He wrapped his thick arms around his body and leaned against the door, which opened suddenly. He stumbled into the cosy warmth of a baker's shop.

'May I have something to eat and somewhere to sleep, just for one night?' he asked the baker.

'Not tonight,' was the reply. 'A fox has crept into one of my ovens. I can't get him out and I won't light the oven with him in there. It would spoil the smell of the bread. I'm too busy sorting this out. Try the butcher. He might help you.'

The baker hurried Alfred out into the cold and set him on his way. When he reached the butcher's shop, he saw through the window a figure standing in darkness. Alfred pushed open the door and stepped inside.

'May I have something to eat and somewhere to sleep, just for one night?' he asked the butcher.

'Not tonight,' was the reply. 'A rat has stolen all of my candles. So I have no light by which to sharpen my knives. If my knives are blunt I cannot cut up the meat. I'm too busy sorting this out. Try the shoemaker. He might help you.'

So Alfred stepped back out into the cold again and went on his way. In the shoemaker's shop he asked once more: 'May I have something to eat and somewhere to sleep, just for one night?'

'Not tonight,' said the shoemaker. 'A magpie has flown off with all of my nails. I need nails to hammer soles on to the shoes. I'm too busy sorting this out. Try the priest. He might help you.'

One last try, thought Alfred as he walked into the church. The priest was busy praying at the altar. Alfred crept up behind him and whispered, 'May I have something to eat and somewhere to sleep, just for one night?'

'Not tonight,' said the priest. 'Tomorrow the bishop is coming and I have an important sermon to write. I have no idea what to say so I'm asking God. I'm too busy sorting this out. Try the farmer. He might help you.'

Alfred gave up. He left the church and sat down by a gravestone. Snow was still falling heavily – the snow angels really did have a nasty side to them. Alfred was upset that no one was kind enough to help him. Why was everyone too busy solving their simple problems? You see, to someone like Alfred problems were easy. When he'd heard that a fox was hiding in the baker's oven, he knew what to do right away. The butcher's candles and the shoemaker's nails could be fixed in a jiffy. And as for the priest's sermon, well now, that was straightforward. Maybe he should go back and tell them his ideas.

Let's create

In *Thinking Stories to Wake up your Mind* (LDA 2007), Alfred gets into trouble for making outrageous snowflakes. In 'Alfred's Gift', we find that he's overstepped the mark once too often and has been banished to Earth. The story provides two big opportunities for creative thinking and problem-solving – Alfred's question snowflakes, and the peculiar problems that he encounters.

Learners will create (over 2 sessions)

1 An Alfred wall inspired by Alfred's trouble-making snowflakes

2 Creative solutions to the four problems in the story

An Alfred wall:

❶ has 3 separate areas
  * for 'How' questions
  * for 'Why' questions
  * for 'What if' questions

❷ has the title 'Alfred's Snowflake Wall'

❸ allows learners to post appropriate questions however they like – e.g.:
  * Using Post-its and pens
  * Adding paper snowflakes with Blu-Tack

❹ grows over time as more questions are added

Creative solutions:

Will be interesting yet plausible courses of action to help the baker, butcher, shoemaker and priest

Learners will develop

An ability to make, think or do things that haven't been made, thought or done before

A belief that creativity can change things and improve things

A belief that mistakes are to be celebrated, learned from and used

A belief that creativity can be a natural response to pain, suffering and boredom

You will need

An Alfred wall plus a few questions of the three different types

Main activity 1

* Share the story up to the end of the third paragraph

* Discuss the questions mentioned in the story; link to the classroom Alfred wall

* Ask learners:
  * Why did Alfred make question snowflakes?
  * What did the people on Earth think of his efforts?
  * What if we could help Alfred to make a questions snowstorm?

* Ask learners to think and talk about the questions that they might put on a snowflake

* Ask them to write questions and place them on the Alfred wall

* Decide how more questions will be placed on the wall – freely / teacher-vetted / as homework, etc.

Main activity 2

- Recap the beginning of the story and read the rest
- Explain that Alfred is also good at creating answers and solutions
- Ask learners to think and then discuss what solutions Alfred might have for the dilemmas he encounters
- Challenge them to find solutions that are linked

Plenary

- Share the various solutions
- Value each solution
- Turn back to Alfred's wall and explain how asking the right questions can lead to solutions
- Ask learners if they:
  - made creative solutions
  - know why Alfred is so creative
  - think their answers to the story problems will help the characters
- Ask learners how they might solve other problems creatively

Support, extension and application

For younger or emerging creators:

- Include a section on the Alfred wall for questions that begin with 'What', 'Who' and 'When'
- Recall other story problems and their solutions
- Give clues and suggestions

For older or more experienced creators:

- Extend the Alfred wall to include questions that begin with 'What else', 'What on Earth', 'Which'

- Set restrictions, such as each solution must include a kettle
- Insist that all 4 solutions are linked

Applications

The Alfred wall may be used to collect questions related to topics or curriculum. Here are some examples of how the baker's problem may be tweaked a little into ones that suggest more subject-specific solutions:

Mathematics

- 'A fox has eaten half of my buns. I have to make some more.'

Language and communication

- 'A talking fox has got stuck in my shop window. He just won't stop going on about how horrible my bread tastes.

Science and technology

- 'A fox has nibbled a piece off every loaf of bread and every cake. My whole stock is ruined. I can't find a way to keep him out.'

Art and design

- 'A fox has got stuck in my shop window. He messed it up so I can no longer advertise and show off my wares.

Health and well-being

- 'A dirty fox has walked all over my bread. It's ruined. I need to find something to sell by this afternoon. There's no time to bake any more bread.'

Human, social and environmental

'A family of foxes from the city keep stealing my bread. I am losing money.'

Click

When the greatest magician in Southwold discovered three lost secrets of the universe, he drew a great deal of unwelcome attention from the science police. He was terrified that his career (and maybe even his life) would come to a messy end if he ever made his findings known to ordinary people. He heard that the police were on their way to Southwold that very day, so he set to work hiding the secrets.

He quickly pushed the first into the spring of a ballpoint pen, the second he wove between the pages of a book, and he dripped the last into a tin of white paint. He rushed to his local shop and placed the pen, the book and the tin of paint on the shelves. After that, just to be on the safe side, he hid himself in the reflections from the window of a nearby bakery. As he vanished into the glass the police turned up.

Over the next few days white-coated men and women roamed around Southwold with clipboards and truncheons. They caused a terrible kerfuffle, beating down doors, asking difficult questions and generally upsetting the residents. Luckily, they didn't find the magician or his secrets.

When they finally packed away their equipment and left, the great magician slid, aching and cold, out of his hiding place and shuffled back to his workshop. He stayed there for many days, waiting for the right time to retrieve the three objects. However, when he finally stepped inside the shop he found that the pen, the book and the tin of paint had all been sold. His face went pale and his body became slack. The secrets were gone – into the hands of people who had no idea of the danger that they now faced.

Let's find the three unlucky people who've bought these things and discover just how much danger they are in.

The Pen

Mrs Gulliver was a very neat and tidy woman. Her house showed no wear on the outside or tear on the inside. The furniture bore no scuffs or chips or scratches, and every item she owned had its special place.

She was obsessed with order and would frequently make lists of what lived where. And if she ever decided to move, say, a chair a little to the left or a vase a little to the right, this had to be noted in a large file.

Mrs Gulliver always recorded items and movements using a black ballpoint pen. Whenever the current pen ran out of ink, she would use her reserve pencil to note this down, then hurry off to buy a new one.

Unbeknownst to Mrs Gulliver, she has just purchased a ballpoint pen whose spring contains one of the world's three lost secrets. What this means is that each time she clicks it in or out, she shrinks in height by one millimetre.

The Book

Foible Carrion loved to read. He loved it so much that he became very ill. He wanted to read every book in the world, but as he couldn't read fast enough to keep up with the new ones that were published, it was a doomed enterprise. Still, nothing and no one had been able to persuade him to try something else.

Foible was ill because he spent every waking hour in the city library, wandering from shelf to shelf, or in the local second-hand book shop, or in his bedroom, hunched over a tiny reading desk.

He was thin and pale and he smelt awful. Such was his obsession.

Unbeknownst to Foible Carrion, he has just purchased a book into whose pages has been woven one of the world's three lost secrets. What this means is that each time he turns a page, the book gets longer by one page. Foible is doomed.

The Paint

Mr Sine the poet lived in a shabby one-room flat. He had very little money, yet he was proud of what he'd achieved in his short and difficult life (two poems published and an article on mildew submitted to Decay Monthly).

Unlike better-known poets he always tried hard to keep himself looking respectable, and worked hard to ensure that his surroundings stayed clean and tidy.

One day he decided to give his one room a makeover. He bought a tin of white paint from the shop and spent the rest of the day moving his four pieces of furniture, two paintings and one small rug around so that he could paint the walls.

As the walls dried and the tangy smell of paint drifted away out of his open window, Mr Sine got ready for bed and slipped under the covers. He spent an unremarkable night and dreamt only once – an unremarkable dream involving three loops of string that kept tangling and untangling.

Unbeknownst to Mr Sine, he has just used a tin of paint into which has been stirred one of the world's three lost secrets. What this means is that his room is now a prison. Each time he attempts to leave through the door, he will find himself coming back in through the window. He can never leave again.

Let's create

Creative problem-solving can be helped by asking the right questions. Asking 'What happens when …?' is a useful prompt for exploring next steps and consequences, and therefore moves us towards solutions. If we ask the question repeatedly we may get nearer and nearer to a good solution.

Learners will create

WHW thinking: a series of responses to the repeated prompt 'What happens when …'

Learners will develop

A belief that creativity can change things and improve things

An attitude of smart risk-taking

A belief that creativity can be a natural response to pain, suffering and boredom

You will need

Nothing

Main activity

- Share the story, allow learners to respond freely, then ask:

  - What was the worst of the 3 fates?

  - Why did the science police act as they did?

  - What if the magician had hidden the secrets somewhere else?

Discuss the consequences for Mrs Gulliver of using her pen – start the discussion by asking for answers to 'What happens when every time she clicks her pen she gets 1 mm smaller?' Record these answers and choose 1

Then use the WHW prompt on the chosen answer – e.g. if the chosen answer is 'She wouldn't notice she was getting smaller at first', ask, 'What happens when she notices?'

Collect answers again, choose 1, then ask WHW? – e.g. if the chosen answer is 'She would try to find out why', ask 'What happens when she realises it's her pen?'

Keep asking WHW? as many times as possible

Apply this method to Foible's book and Mr Sine's room

Plenary

- Think about if and how the WHW thinking process helps in understanding a difficult problem
- Ask learners if they:
  - have learned more about solving problems
  - took a risk in their thinking
  - believe that creative thinking helps solve problems
- Record their comments publicly where they can be referred to easily

Support, extension and application

For younger or emerging creators:

- Ask 'What happens next?' once
- Give real examples of what did happen when …
- Prompt with familiar events – e.g. What happens when … it rains?

For older or more experienced creators:

- Challenge learners to repeat the WHW process 7 times
- Use the prompt 'What doesn't happen when …'
- Ask learners to rank/order the different responses to a WHW prompt

Applications

The WHW thinking process may be applied to specific curriculum areas and problems related to them:

Mathematics

- WHW the answer doesn't feel right?

Language and communication

- WHW the conversation dries up?

Science and technology

- WHW the experiment doesn't work?

Art and design

- WHW the product isn't fit for purpose?

Health and well-being

- WHW we eat 5 pieces of fruit and vegetables a day?

Human, social and environmental

- WHW a tanker spills oil into the sea?

The Boy who built

There once was a boy who built wonderful things: houses made of purple bricks shaped like diamonds, quirky hotels with walls full of tiny round windows and rooms carved out of rubber, grand old churches crammed with golden ornaments and topped off with twisting glittering spires that reached high into the sky. He also built tiny machines that clicked and whirred and big ones that shuddered and juddered and hooted. Then, when he'd done this, he laid out sunlit gardens with meandering paths and statues hidden behind curly bamboo and tall dark hedges. And sometimes, but not too often, he built very dangerous creatures: Fovvel Wands, Crake Breakers, Jooble Slicks and occasionally the most hazardous ones of all: Drool Dragons.

All day long he constructed and concocted, he invented and cemented. He fashioned and formed and joined and glued and linked and pressed into place. And when he was done, there wasn't a single thing to show for it (in the real world, that is) because all this went on inside his head.

Then, like a cloud slipping in front of the sun, it was time for him to start going to school.

On the first day he sat behind an enormous wooden desk and tried in vain to listen to his teacher. She was droning on about rules and words and behaviour and verbs. He tried to understand what she said but the sounds just couldn't get in. They tried, but they were turned away like waves breaking against a sea wall. So he went back to his building.

On the second day she spoke for three hours about numbers and dates and lining up and mistakes but still it made no sense. His ears repelled the sounds like opposite magnetic poles. So he went back to his building.

On the third day he went to his building first – before she launched into a speech about full stops. But he was spotted, staring out of the window. He was in the middle of assembling a grand suspension bridge swooping down like thick orange brush strokes over a deep blue river full of sparkling silver fish. He was made to stand at the front of the class and explain why he hadn't been listening. The other children smiled and grinned, glad to be safe and sound behind their enormous wooden desks. He didn't know what to say and his bridge faded and his blue river ran dry.

On the fourth day he had to stand outside the classroom. Teachers passing by made tutting noises and shook their heads. A tear grew in his right eye, swelled and then splashed on to the floor. He was made to wipe it up by a particularly fussy cleaner. And his churches crumbled and his towers fell to the ground.

On the fifth day it was outside the headmaster's office for him. 'He simply refuses to listen, always staring out of the window; how rude, how naughty, how unacceptable,' his teacher had said. The secretaries and school visitors raised their eyebrows at him as they walked by. How dare someone disrupt the talking of a teacher by looking out of the window? Both his eyes bulged with tears this time, and the drops of salty water made damp patches on the carpet. And in his head the machines jammed and fell apart and the gardens grew dark and overgrown.

And on the sixth day he got to stand inside the headmaster's room, together with his teacher, his parents and a man called Mr Locus who knew all about children's heads – which was surprising because he had not been a child for many years. Possibly he'd read about them in a book somewhere. The grown-ups looked at him with a sadness that made the last of his buildings collapse and all his creatures run away.

It was decided that he was a boy with a slow brain. A brain that was to be pitied and patronised. A brain that wasn't built for listening. Mr Locus had come across a good many cases such as this and he knew what would be best for all concerned. And it may even be good for the boy as well.

He was sent away to a school for children with slow brains, brains that were not fast enough for real school, brains that preferred building to listening. In his new school there was just as much droning, but it was slower and softer. The sounds moved like feathers drifting down on to marshmallows, but still they came nowhere near him.

For seven years he stared out of the window in his classroom in the school for children with slow brains, but his head stayed empty of building. He couldn't even imagine one brick on top of another.

And then he became a man and it was time to go out into the world.

For seven more years he sat in an office in front of a large pile of papers, and still he stared out of the window, waiting.

But one day something happened. He was staring at the building opposite when he caught sight of a woman sitting at a desk in front of a pile of papers, staring in his direction and smiling. He was sure she wanted to tell him something so he smiled back.

Now, years later, there's a wise and very rich old man who builds the most wonderful things: houses made of burgundy and ochre bricks, quirky hotels full of tiny windows and topped off with twisting chimneys, grand old churches crammed with golden ornaments and glittering jewelled towers reaching high into the sky. He also builds tiny machines that click and whirr and big ones that shudder and judder and hoot. Then, when he's done this, he lays out sunlit gardens with meandering paths and statues hidden behind curly bamboo and tall dark hedges. And sometimes, but not too often, he builds very dangerous creatures: Fovvel Wands, Crake Breakers, Jooble Slicks and the most hazardous ones of all: Drool Dragons.

Let's create

Thankfully, we educators are always on the look out for children like the one in the story. Or we should be. If his teacher valued creativity, then the boy who built would have thrived.

Children (and adults) need a learning community in which their ideas, however wacky, will be listened to and respected, and receive a warm, non-judgemental response. We need principles and expected behaviours for such an environment, and they need to be developed with the children, not imposed upon them:

Learners will create

A class creativity charter (a 'Triple C') that describes what should go on in a classroom where creativity is encouraged.

Learners will develop

A belief that creative potential is inside everyone

An attitude of non-judgement

You will need

Flipchart paper and pens

Main activity

- Share the story, allow learners to respond freely, then ask:
  - Why did the boy struggle in school?
  - What happened to him after he saw the woman?
  - What if his school had been different?

- Ask learners to discuss what sort of classroom the boy would have liked.
  - Ask the following questions:
  ❶ What do we see in this classroom when we are being creative?
  ❷ What do we hear in this classroom when we are being creative?
  ❸ What do we feel in the classroom when we are being creative?
  ❹ What can get in the way of us being creative?

Respond to these prompts through a carousel activity

Carousel

Small groups (or pairs/individuals) have a few minutes each to answer 1 of the questions written on a flipchart

Each group then moves on to the next question, ticking answers which they strongly agree with and adding more ideas as they are able

When all groups have answered all questions, they return to their first question and decide on 1 or 2 answers to go forward as the success criteria for a creative classroom community

When groups have reported back, the chosen ideas are displayed and become a working document

These suggestions are then used as lesson objectives and assessment criteria; as a result they will be defined and refined further

Remember that as the teacher you are part of the creative community, so do add things to the list that children may have missed – but please don't copy this example to save time as your learners won't have any buy-in if you present them with a *fait accompli*.

Typical set of ideas

In our creative classroom we hear:

- people saying things like 'What would happen if?', 'What would it be like if?'
- people saying things like 'That's interesting, tell me more'
- laughter and jokes
- people clapping others' ideas

In our creative classroom we see:

- people learning on their own, in pairs and in different groups
- people using lots of different tools and materials
- people building and making

In our creative classroom we feel:

- excited to be creating new things
- respected when we talk about our ideas
- able to make mistakes and try out new ways of doing things

In our creative classroom we try to avoid:

- saying if someone's idea or creation is right or wrong
- doing the same thing in the same way every time
- answers – we prefer questions

Plenary

- Call these principles the Triple C, and ask learners to try their best to follow them
- Ask learners how judgement and mistakes can affect creativity
- Ask them whether some people are more creative than others
- Hold on to these themes as your creative environment grows

Support, extension and application

For younger or emerging creators:

- Gather ideas over a longer period of time
- Give examples of the features of a creative environment

For older or more experienced creators:

- Evaluate and refine your Triple C
- Collect examples of each principle

Applications

The carousel process may be applied in other ways. Here are some ideas for what the question themes might be:

Mathematics

- Solving multi-part problems

Language and communication

- Generating word/idea banks to make writing more engaging

Science and technology

- Agreeing safe behaviours around tools, materials and chemicals

Art and design

- Making responses to artwork

Health and well-being

- Describing a healthy lifestyle

Human, social and environmental

- Planning a school trip

Ghramo's Mountain

It was early evening on the bitterest day of winter when Ghramo decided to climb the mountain. Snow was falling as if the gods were having a vicious pillow fight, and the wind was an icy hand trying to push Ghramo back down to his village.

Ghramo wanted to talk to the wise man who lived at the top of the mountain. His elderly parents had warned him not to go out in this terrible weather. His friends had told him of the dangers and his wife had begged him to stay by the fire in their tiny cottage. But Ghramo was determined: he had a question for the wise man and it couldn't wait a day longer.

Ghramo's mouth was set and his eyes were slits against the blasts of freezing air. As the day darkened, his steps became slower and he sank deeper into the snow. It was exhausting to pull his legs up and out, then push them back down, moving only a few centimetres forward for all that effort. It was gruelling to do it again and again, and disheartening that with each step the snow level rose higher and higher. But he had his question and the wise man would tell him the answer.

He was halfway up when the terrible thing happened. He stopped – not just for a rest but completely. Ghramo stopped utterly and absolutely. His heart stopped. His brain stopped. His legs and his arms and his feet stopped as well as his fingers and toes and lungs and kidneys and liver. Everything came to a frozen halt. But Ghramo hadn't died. He'd just iced up in mid-stride and now stood there like a statue. The snow built up around him and before long he was buried under a small white mound.

The villagers waited, and when he didn't return the following day, and the next, they feared the worst. After six days even his wife accepted that Ghramo must have died on his foolhardy journey. On the seventh day, when it stopped snowing and still he didn't return, she let out a howl that echoed all around the valley.

The sound startled birds and caused deer to stop in their tracks. It spread across the forest and vibrated around the mountain where her husband stood, motionless and hidden. There was so much pain and energy in her wailing that it disturbed the freshly laid snow, and before long an avalanche began to rumble down the mountain side. Clumps of ice and rock hurtled towards the rise that concealed Ghramo's body. One piece hit him right in the middle and smashed him into seven pieces. Each piece disappeared under the roaring landslide that followed.

The days passed and the weeks turned winter into spring. Gradually the snow on the mountain melted away. In the warm air Ghramo's body appeared once more, the seven pieces scattered where the avalanche had carried them. As new life began to appear from the ground, something strange happened to Ghramo: very very slowly, each piece started to change. An arm grew a new body, head and legs; the head sprouted a body, arms and legs; on to an old leg grew a new body, arms, head and another leg. Each of the seven pieces grew into a brand-new Ghramo. Little by little each Ghramo came to life. The parts that had stopped so suddenly last winter began to work again.

Months passed, but as soon as the seven Ghramos sat up for the first time a snowflake fluttered from the sky. Winter had come back when they finally stood up. But instead of walking down to the village, they set off *up* the mountain. Each new Ghramo was as determined as the original one to ask the wise man their question. Once again the snows and the wind rushed towards them. Each one struggled to keep going, but at last all seven stopped and froze up as Ghramo had done the year before.

It was the anniversary of the very day when Ghramo's wife had finally accepted his death. Down in the village she let out a cry of mourning as she remembered him. Once again it rattled through the valley. Once again its energy dislodged the snow and another avalanche was set off. This time, as it tumbled down the mountain, each of the frozen Ghramos was shattered into seven more pieces that lay buried until the spring sun returned.

By next winter forty-nine Ghramos were making their stubborn way up towards the wise man.

For many years this continued. Every winter more and more Ghramos were caught in a snow storm, froze and were broken by the avalanche, itself caused by the first Ghramo's loving wife. Each year they got closer to the top. Each year the climb grew more crowded.

The wise man had been watching this with interest. He marvelled at the determination of the first man, then the seven, the forty-nine and now the thousands who were busy tramping towards him. It was ten years since Ghramo's journey began, but all of them were as single-minded as the first.

Eventually there we so many Ghramos that the annual avalanche wasn't strong enough to break them. In fact they stopped it from tumbling any farther down the mountain. Very quickly, all the Ghramos reached the top of the mountain and gathered around the wise man's hut. He poked his head round the door and smiled at them. 'Yes?' he said.

'We have a question for you,' they responded as one. 'We should like to know why men are so stubborn, why they don't listen to advice, and why they are so determined.'

'Ah,' said the wise man, 'I believe that you already know the answer. Tell me, what drove you all to complete your journey here?'

'We wanted to know,' they replied, 'we wanted to know ...'

See pp. 26 and 27 for the activities relating to this story.

Four Wits of the Irish

A oife (pronounced ee-fa) and Ronan were head over heels in love and soon to be married. So deep was their love that everyone and everything else was forgotten. They lived in a world of their own. From dawn till dusk they walked in the forest holding hands and staring into each other's eyes. All summer they strolled through dusty shafts of golden sunlight, sighing in admiration at each other's beauty and giggling at whispered jokes. It was all quite sickening really, and I can forgive you for feeling just a tiny bit pleased about the misfortune that soon came upon them.

During a particularly tight embrace that included a rather long kiss, Aoife and Ronan slowly became aware of someone watching them from behind a tree. They gasped as a small and hideous woman stepped out of the shadows and limped towards them. She wore a twisted smile and carried a worryingly large pair of scissors.

'Ah! Sweet lovers,' she croaked, 'spare a lock of your shining hair so that old Marta can share in your happiness.' Snip, snip, snip went old Marta's scissors as she took a step towards Aoife. In a flash Ronan, brave in love though short of temper, jumped between them and shouted.

'Old hag, your ugliness would turn ripe fruit rotten, send children scampering behind their mothers' skirts and keep the stars from twinkling at night! Why on this Earth should you share in our blessed love? No hair from my Aoife's head shall come near your foul body!' He shoved the old woman to the ground and spat on her.

He expected her to grovel for forgiveness, but instead she sat right up and began to cackle, 'Oh, foolish boy, one lock of hair has cost you the whole head!' With that Marta sprang towards Aoife, touched her arm, and they both disappeared. Ronan had deeply offended a very highly born (if very ugly) fairy.

A distraught young Ronan stumbled back home and, between sobs, explained to his parents what had happened. They told him to visit Crionna the druid, who would know exactly what to do. Crionna had skills and wisdom from the old times that gave him power over fairies like Marta. But he didn't offer his help willingly; it had to be earned.

So Ronan found himself sitting in Crionna's tiny hut, warming his bones by an enormous fire and listening carefully as the old druid explained the three tasks that he must complete before Aoife would be set free.

'Firstly, Ronan, you must steal the golden ring that the bishop wears on his left hand. Secondly, I want you to find out why our river runs dry each spring. And, lastly, you must serve a beggar.'

Ronan started to protest (particularly about task number 3), but Crionna held up his hand. 'If you truly love Aoife as much as you say, then these three tasks will be a joyous toil to you for each day will bring her freedom a little closer. You have the wits to succeed, Ronan!'

Well now, the shock of losing his wife-to-be and the daunting tasks he'd been given could have turned a man like Ronan into a moaning, whining boy. But a quiet confidence came to him.

He did love Aoife and he *would* get her back! He set off for the bishop's palace at once.

On the way he came upon a pathetic-looking bundle of rags by the side of the road. 'Spare a coin, sir, for one of God's children?' came a whisper from the rags.

Ronan replied, 'I'll spare you more than a coin. Your bidding is my delight.'

At first the beggar thought Ronan was playing a cruel trick on him, but when he asked Ronan to carry him to the river for a drink Ronan did as he was bid. The beggar gained faith in him. Once they were at the river bank Ronan asked the beggar, 'How may I serve you next?'

'Oh, kind sir, you have already. I've been ignored for years, so when you noticed me and carried me here I began to exist again. Just set me down for a while. I will drink from the river while it still runs and then continue my rest.'

'You know why the river runs dry each spring?' asked Ronan quickly.

'I know where the answer lies,' the beggar replied. 'The grey scholars will tell you.'

Ronan had completed one of Crionna's tasks, and as he looked at the old man a plan to accomplish the others grew in his mind.

'Old man, it is becoming cold here by the river. Let us exchange clothes. Mine are thick and heavy, yours are light and worn. I am setting off for the bishop's palace and the walk will keep me warm.

So they dressed in each other's garments and Ronan continued on his way to the palace. At the gates he was admitted at once. Beggars were always welcomed by the bishop. He took bread and wine, then asked to speak to the bishop.

'Your grace, I am just a poor beggar, but I dream of making a better life for myself. I wish to study with the grey scholars. I will then devote my mind to the service of others.'

The bishop had never heard a beggar speak with such determination and hope, so he told Ronan that he must go to the scholars and that the church would pay for his learning.

'But, your grace, how will the scholars know that it is you who has sent me?'

'Why, here is the ring from my left hand. It will vouch for you!'

Ronan left the palace and headed to the college of the grey scholars. At first they were suspicious of this beggar and his claims, but the sight of the bishop's ring quickly changed their minds.

Ronan was given a room and began his studies the next day. The scholars were most impressed with their new student. He was eager to learn and he progressed swiftly during the next six months. He took a special interest in rivers. He became an expert on how they carved their way through valleys and why sometimes they flooded or dried up.

The scholars were surprised and saddened one day to discover that Ronan had left the college and could be found nowhere in the neighbouring buildings or fields.

Ronan, of course, was back in Crionna's hut. He stood there smiling in his beggar's clothes, held out the bishop's ring, and told Crionna why the river dried up each spring. Crionna asked him to step outside the hut. He did so, and there was Aoife, waiting for him with tears in her eyes.

Let's create

Irish folklore is shot through with many valuable types of intelligence. For example, Crionna has the wisdom of age, Ronan is shrewd and cunning, while the grey scholars demonstrate intellectual strength. Varied creative responses to this story will help learners understand these different faculties.

Learners will create

An original and simplified 7-part retelling of the story in a choice of media

Learners will develop

An attitude of smart risk-taking

An ability to make, think or do things that haven't been made, thought or done before

An ability to see familiar things in new and different ways

You will need

A range of tools, materials and media to support the simplified creative retelling of the story. – e.g. art materials, musical instruments, digital camera, computer

Main activity

- Share the story, allow learners to respond freely, then ask:
  - What was Ronan's cleverest action?
  - Why did Crionna set Ronan 3 tasks?
  - What if Ronan had been polite to the fairy?
- Ask your learners to retell the story to each other
- Together summarise the key events of the story
- Ask in what other ways stories can be told (film, animation, written, comic, etc.)
- Challenge your learners to retell the story in exactly 7 stages, choosing 1 of the following ways:
  - sounds
  - stick drawings
  - sentences
  - posed scenes, photographed
  - pieces of clip-art
  - speech bubbles
  - Play/Plasticine models
  - lines of a poem
  - questions
  - stages of a flowchart

Plenary

- Share the various retellings and compare how well they each represent the key parts of the story

- Consider which form of retelling is most useful

- Discuss whether the limit of 7 stages helped or hindered retelling the story

- Ask learners if they:

  - took a risk

  - made something new

  - gained a better understanding of the story

- Record their comments publicly where they can be referred to easily

Support, extension and application

For younger or emerging creators:

- Ask learners to retell 1 or 2 favourite moments from the story

- Provide 4 or 5 stages in 1 form – e.g. stick drawings – and ask them to fill in the gaps

- Ask learners to retell a recently experienced event in 1 of the forms

For older or more experienced creators:

- Retell the story in 3 or 10 stages

- Retell the story in 2 or 3 mixed forms – e.g. stick drawings and sounds

- Rearrange the 7 stages and retell this altered story

Applications

The world's knowledge doubles every six months or so and is speeding up. Today's learners need effective skills to access, process and express vast amounts of information. Re-presenting knowledge as seven key points is one way to cut through this enormous and growing pile of facts.

Certain aspects of curriculum subjects lend themselves to this type of distillation and re-presentation:

Mathematics
- 7 trickiest tables facts

Language and communication
- 7 most useful words

Science and technology
- 7 hardest materials

Art and design
- 7 best paintings

Health and well-being
- 7 most enjoyable sports

Human, social and environmental
- 7 most significant dates in history

The Trouble with Wishes

Walking home from school one day, Uki had the misfortune to step on a wish devil. The tiny red creature popped open under her foot. She felt its delicate legs crunch and heard its little coiled back snap in two. This was all over in a second, but for the next few minutes she watched in horror as it squirmed and writhed and then finally became still and died.

Uki was frozen with fear and braced herself for what was to come. It was well known that the soul of a wish devil, released on death, would bring great trouble upon the nearest living thing. Sure enough, a grey mist began to emerge from the corpse and swirled around Uki's legs. It spread upwards, thickening and curling around her body and she was soon completely engulfed. Then, with a sound like a thousand teachers going 'Shh', Uki and the mist disappeared!

Uki found herself standing in a street that wasn't quite a street, in a city that wasn't quite a city, and in a dim not quite light. Tall buildings twisted and arched around her, the top floors splitting open and dividing like the branches of great black trees. Every window in the buildings was skewed, every door deformed. Shop fronts were crooked, signposts bent out of shape and benches warped. Nothing in this place was right. Everything was distorted.

There were people here too. They looked normal but they were acting strangely. Each person was in a world of their own. Some were shuffling about with their heads down and muttering to themselves. Others were standing totally still, staring into the distance with slight frowns upon their brows, as if trying to solve some simple yet elusive problem. Even more were shouting angrily into the air. As one approached Uki, she realised what they were doing. They were all making wishes.

'I wish I was rich!', 'I wish I was back home!', 'I wish my enemies were dead!', 'I wish for a banquet!', 'I wish for a wife!', 'I wish to live forever!' – it was a desperate cacophony of pleading and demanding. It went on and on, and each time a wish was made something did happen, but not what Uki would have expected. When one woman wished to be rich, she instantly turned to gold from her neck down. To undo this disaster she wished to be poor, and immediately became sick and weak and wretchedly thin, and suffered everything that came along with being poor in a place like this.

One man wished to be handsome. Right away he turned into a carriage, a horse-drawn Hansom carriage, and was pulled away along the road. Hurriedly he wished to be plain and you can guess what happened.

Wish devils' souls had brought Uki and these people to a corrupted place where all wishes came true, but never in the way that the wisher wanted. People were trapped here, desperately trying to

114

fulfil their dreams or to escape, but they couldn't find the words they needed. They couldn't make the right wish, and their words were interpreted in devious and mischievous ways. Uki would have to be very careful what she wished for if she was ever to get home.

She listened carefully to what the others were saying and, before long, she worked out a pattern. People began with greedy wishes to make themselves into someone better or to get something they didn't have. When this went wrong, they tried to undo the mistake with what they thought was the reverse wish. But that just got them into deeper trouble. Soon, when things were about as bad as they could get, they frantically wished to go back to wherever they had come from. But that failed too. Wishes like 'I wish I was at home' took the wisher to some random home, possibly the home of a giraffe or a beetle, or maybe of a family of worms. 'I wish I was in my home' was no better. The wisher certainly went to their home, but as it was years in the past or would be in the future. After some thought they came up with, 'I wish I was exactly where I was – same place and time – before I was brought here.' They did indeed go back as requested, but they were immediately whisked away again because, of course, they had no time to run away from the wish devil on which they had just trodden.

Uki listened and Uki thought. Uki tried out different wishes in her mind and predicted what might happen. Uki pondered, mused, created, wondered, experimented and finally decided on the one wish that would release her from this place. She took a deep breath, gathered her wish and cried out, 'I wish that wish devils had never existed, and never will.'

And all of a sudden Uki was walking home from school and didn't know a thing about what she'd just done.

Let's create

They just couldn't make the right wish; their words were interpreted in devious and mischievous ways

A wish chain is a wonderful technique for exploring existing ideas and for creating new ones. The people in the story make wish chains: wish after wish after wish, each one getting them further from what they really want. A wish chain copies this process in a different context.

Learners will create

A wish chain of linked ideas

Learners will develop

An ability to make, think or do things that haven't been made, thought or done before

A belief that mistakes are to be celebrated, learned from and used

An attitude of positivity towards surprising and unexpected events

You will need

Strips of paper and glue/tape for making paper chains

Main activity

- Share the story, allow learners to respond freely, then ask:
  - What did Uki do that was a mistake?
  - Why do people wish for things?
  - What if Uki's wish hadn't worked?
- Ask learners to pair up
- Demonstrate how to link strips of paper together into a chain

- Explain the process for making a wish chain like the ones in the story:
  - first person makes a simple wish: 'I wish ...' (write it on the first strip of paper and loop it)
  - second person decides how the wish is not quite granted: 'I grant you ...' (write this on a second strip and link to the first)
  - first person makes another wish to try to put things right (write this on another strip of paper and join it on)
  - second person responds
  - continue the chain until 7 wishes have been not quite granted

Some ideas to start with

- I wish for an underground house
- I wish I were a wizard
- I wish I lived on another planet
- I wish the trees could talk
- I wish I could smell colours and taste sounds
- I wish I could sleep all day
- I wish for war to end
- I wish for a huge bar of chocolate
- I wish for all shouting to stop
- I wish I were happy all the time
- I wish for a really long holiday by the sea
- I wish I had a dog

Example

- I wish I had a dog
- I grant you a fierce dog that can't be trained
- I wish my dog were really friendly
- I grant your dog to be so friendly that he annoys strangers

116

- I wish my dog didn't annoy strangers
- I grant that your dog sleeps all day so he can't annoy strangers
- I wish my dog were normal
- I grant that your dog is now average and boring
- I wish I had a different pet
- I grant you a giraffe
- I wish my pet were smaller
- I grant you a 2 cm giraffe
- I wish my giraffe were a cat
- I grant you a cat with a 3 m long neck

Plenary

- Present and evaluate the wish chains, looking for
  - creative wishes and outcomes
  - humour
  - shrewd links
  - new ideas emerging
- Ask learners if they:
  - had new thoughts
  - behaved in a positive way when their wish went wrong
  - accepted and learned from their wish mistakes

Support, extension and application

For younger or emerging creators:

- Make single wish loops (no responses) and link them together
- Look for wishes in familiar stories
- Share your own wishes

For older or more experienced creators:

- Attempt to link the wish chain back to itself by making the last wish the same as the first
- Work in 3s and allow 2 people not quite to grant the wish in different ways
- Relate the initial wish to large-scale global issues

Applications

Wish chains can be used to explore different topic areas creatively. Here are some 'I wish' prompts that can be used to begin the chain process:

Mathematics
- I wish I could remember 100 digits in order

Language and communication
- I wish I knew every word in my language

Science and technology
- I wish robots did all the chores

Art and design
- I wish I were a great artist

Health and well-being
- I wish I were a famous tennis player

Human, social and environmental
- I wish I could travel in time

The Smallest Story on Earth

The Fourth Smallest Story on Earth

There once lived a young boy who was very poor. He collected together some food and the few things he owned, and set out on the road to seek his fortune. But a bandit was laying in wait and when the boy passed by he was attacked. The bandit took his food and his possessions and left the boy for dead. When the boy came to, he discovered that he had dashed his head on a rock. There was blood everywhere. He looked at the rock and was amazed to see a gigantic emerald stuck there. So he levered it out, took it home and was rich for the rest of his days.

The Third Smallest Story on Earth

A poor young boy packed some food and set out to seek his fortune. But a bandit attacked him, took his food and left him for dead. When the boy awoke he saw blood from his head on a nearby rock. When he looked closer, though, he was amazed to see a gigantic emerald stuck in the rock. So he levered it out and was rich for the rest of his days.

The Second Smallest Story on Earth

The Smallest Story on Earth

118

Let's create

This basic story motif may be made more concise or more detailed. The process, once learned, can be used as a thinking tool for investigating ideas.

Learners will create

Zoom in and out of the story.

Learners will develop

An ability to use both analytic and holistic thinking

An ability to see familiar things in new and different ways

A belief that creativity can change things and improve things

You will need

Copies of the story (downloadable from www.thinkingclassroom.co.uk)

Main activity

- Share the stories, allow learners to respond, then ask:
  - What is the story's meaning?
  - Why can the story get smaller and still make sense?
  - What if we could write the smallest story on Earth?
- Provide copies of the stories. Ask learners to zoom in to the story:
  - highlight the key points of the 'Third Smallest story on Earth'
  - decide if all of them are needed
  - discard those that aren't
  - using what's left, write the 'Second Smallest Story on Earth'
- Zoom further to get the 'Smallest Story'

Plenary

- Compare the various versions
- Ask learners if they:
  - were able to zoom
  - changed their view of the story
- Record their comments publicly

Support, extension and application

For younger or emerging creators:

- Provide a version of the second smallest or smallest story and ask them for the 2 or 3 main features
- Re-present the story as pictures

For older or more experienced creators:

- Zoom out – write the fifth and sixth smallest stories
- Define clear criteria for keeping or discarding a key point

Applications

Zooming in to an idea may help learners to explore its component parts; zooming out provides a view of the idea in context. Here are some ideas to zoom in and out of:

Mathematics
- A range of measurements

Language and communication
- A poem

Science and technology
- An egg

Art and design
- A famous painting

Health and well-being
- A meal

Human, social and environmental
- A friendship

The Golden Steps in 16 Pieces

A young girl	Wanting to see distant lands	Seeking gold!	Setting out with bread, cheese and water
A flight of steps	Feeling curious	A golden staircase	Climbing higher and higher
Feeling richer and greedier	Desperate to reach the top	Stuck at the top	Growing very angry
Trying and trying to keep going	Kicking	The staircase vanishes	No way down ...

Ghramo's Mountain in 16 pieces

Bitterest day of winter	Snow and icy wind	Ghramo decides to climb the mountain	Seeking the wise man
Ignores advice to stay indoors	Fighting the snow, slower and slower	Wanting to ask the wise man a question	He stops ands freezes solid
Buried under the snow	He must be dead!	An avalanche is coming	Ghramo is smashed into 7 pieces
7 Ghramos come alive and begin to climb	They all freeze and are each smashed into 7 pieces	Thousands of Ghramos reach the wise man	'Why are men so stubborn?'

Crazy Challenge Table

Pick an item from each column

In column 3 decide exactly what the item is; for example: any tool – pair of pliers; any vegetable – potato

A difficult journey	Who/what goes on the journey	Items to help on the journey
Crossing a river	A bottle of milk	Any tool
Through a rabbit warren	A bag of money	Any small animal
To the bottom of the sea	A hamster in a cage	Any musical instrument
Across the desert	A box of eggs	Any vegetable
Across the frozen lake	A paper bag full of flour	Any loud noise
Over the mountains	A cup of water	Any piece of furniture
Over a rope bridge	A burning candle	Any piece of clothing

Crazy Challenge Table

Pick an item from each column

In column 3 decide exactly what the item is; for example: any tool – pair of pliers; any vegetable – potato

A difficult journey	Who/what goes on the journey	Items to help on the journey
Crossing a river	A bottle of milk	Any tool
Through a rabbit warren	A bag of money	Any small animal
To the bottom of the sea	A hamster in a cage	Any musical instrument
Across the desert	A box of eggs	Any vegetable
Across the frozen lake	A paper bag full of flour	Any loud noise
Over the mountains	A cup of water	Any piece of furniture
Over a rope bridge	A burning candle	Any piece of clothing

Chevalier Board

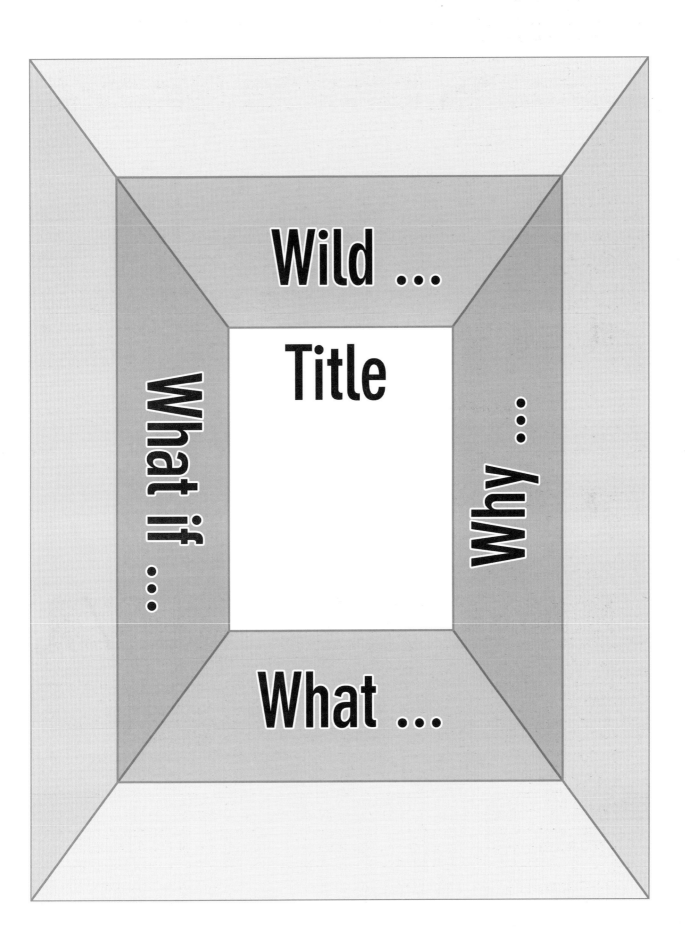

How to Create 101 Interesting Questions

Prompts and examples	Questions
Senses	
Sight – What had the soldier seen?	
Sound – What was the angel's voice like?	
Smell – What smells came from Reuben's lunchbox?	
Taste – What does battlefield mud taste like?	
Touch – What texture does a devil's skin have?	
Time	
Past – Where did the old man come from?	
Present – What time is it when Reuben sets out?	
Future – Where will the characters be in 100 years?	
Ways of thinking	
Music – What sounds happen in the story?	
Words – Which words are most useful in the story?	
Deep – Why do people ask 'Who am I?'?	
Nature – Where does the story take place?	
People – What others could the boy ask?	
Logic – What happens if the order of events is changed?	
Movement – What if all the characters in the story could fly?	
Pictures – What if the characters' thoughts became visible?	
Feeling – How was each character feeling?	
Creative changes	
Add – Which character from another story could you add?	
Remove – Who or what could you remove from the story?	
Reverse – What if the others asked the boy who they were?	
Combine – What if the angel and devil appeared as one character?	
Miscellaneous	
Points of view – What did the tree see?	
Dig deeper – What was in the boy's tin?	
Comparing – Which character is best?	
Space – How far did each character travel?	
Oddball – What would happen if a telephone rang?	
Format – How would the story work as a radio show?	

Medicine Bottles

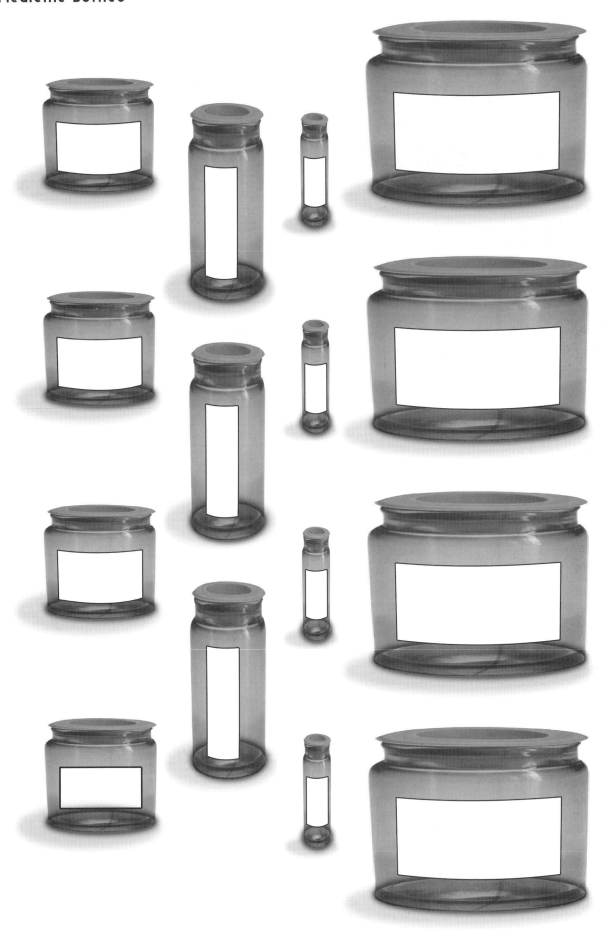

Curious Childhood Illnesses

Cortex cough

Whatever the child is thinking about at the point of coughing springs to life in front of them

Cross-mutus

When the child attempts to speak they can only sing; when they attempt to sing they can only draw; when they attempt to draw they can only mime; when they attempt to mime they can only speak

Sunday fever

A hot flush occurring only between the hours of 7 and 8 p.m. on a Sunday

Croats

Arm swellings that prevent the removal of a coat in summer

Throat weaver

A three-legged voice beetle that removes all words from a teenager apart from 'Uhhh' and 'Whatever'

Hubert's spikes / Hubert's spines

Whenever the child becomes angry, a spike erupts from their body, its proportions matching the intensity of the anger

Nerve stones

Tiny blue pebbles that collect at the base of the neck and spine, one for each shock the child has received

Christmas blotch

An unusual and uneven swelling of the child when it mistakenly experiences the excitement of Christmas Eve on behalf of 20 other children, all at once

Christmas stoop

An unusual and uneven shrinking of the child on experiencing no excitement on Christmas Eve

Carper's stockets

The appearance of sticky balls of hair, cat fur, sofa fluff and boiled sweets on the skull. They enlarge and work their way down the head as the hair to which they cling grows. If attempts are made to remove them by cutting, soaking or pulling, stockets will enlarge and grip tighter.

Brithy's skin tangle

If two children with Brithy's syndrome should touch skin to skin, their skins seek each other out and begin to mix and flow

Time flu

Whenever the patient sneezes, they jump back one minute in time

Angelica poxa (angel blight)

Seen in children who perform too many good deeds or who tell too many tales – their skin (usually around the knees and palms) breaks out in large red angel-shaped boils

Nibbets

An infestation of louse-like parasites whose bodies ooze coloured ink. They leave coloured trails as they wander across the skin. The trails must not be picked off and will fade after several days. Some attacks of nibbets produce rude words.

Spine stix

Children who lay down to rest on dried reetle sticks in a forest find that any movement of the spine thereafter results in very loud crackling and snapping, as of dry twigs being walked on

Alien Creator Grid

<table>
<tr><td colspan="2">1st dice</td><td></td><td></td><td></td><td></td><td></td></tr>
<tr><td></td><td>1</td><td>2</td><td>3</td><td>4</td><td>5</td><td>6</td></tr>
<tr><td>1</td><td>Is egg shaped</td><td>Is oily</td><td>Is shiny and metallic</td><td>Is polished like wood</td><td>Has one or more wheels</td><td>Has a boiler</td></tr>
<tr><td>2</td><td>Has 2 or more gears</td><td>Is sleek and white</td><td>Is covered in flickering lights</td><td>Is covered in colourful lights</td><td>Has 2 or more flashing screens</td><td>Has 2 arms with tools on the ends</td></tr>
<tr><td>3</td><td>Has 2 legs with tools on the ends</td><td>Has 3 or more joints</td><td>Is mainly grey</td><td>Has a part that is boiling</td><td>Has a part that is squirming</td><td>Gives off black smoke</td></tr>
<tr><td>4</td><td>Makes a rattling sound</td><td>Can be ridden by an Avanian</td><td>Can drill deep underground</td><td>Can plant crops</td><td>Can float</td><td>Can erect buildings</td></tr>
<tr><td>5</td><td>Can disappear into an Avanian's brain</td><td>Can control an Avanian's body and mind</td><td>Is clumpy and lumpy</td><td>Is mainly black</td><td>Is part wooden</td><td>Vapour comes off it</td></tr>
<tr><td>6</td><td>Has an outer casing</td><td>Has a special leg</td><td>Can create food from waste</td><td>Has a special tool</td><td>Has a rusty part</td><td>Connects to itself</td></tr>
</table>

2nd dice (vertical label for rows)

Shake 2 dice 6 times to discover the features that your alien must have:

Feature 1: ....

Feature 2: ....

Feature 3: ....

Feature 4: ....

Feature 5: ....

Feature 6: ....

Extra 1: ....

Extra 2: ....

or

Rethrow 1: ....

Mash-up Poem Grid

	See	Hear	Taste	Touch	Smell
Image:					
Sound:					
Flavour:					
Texture:					
Aroma:					

Mash-up Poem Grid

	See	Hear	Taste	Touch	Smell
Image:					
Sound:					
Flavour:					
Texture:					
Aroma:					